WITH GOD IN RED CHINA

WITH GOD IN RED CHINA

The true story of a group of uncompromising
Christians courageously surviving under communism.

MARY WANG

DIMENSION BOOKS
BETHANY FELLOWSHIP, INC.
Minneapolis, Minnesota

With God in Red China
Originally published under the title
God's School in Red China.
by Mary Wang

Library of Congress Catalog Card
Number 77-78610

ISBN Number 0-87123-186-7

This edition published in 1977 by special arrangement with
Hodder and Stoughton Limited, London.

DIMENSION BOOKS
Bethany Fellowship, Inc.
6820 Auto Club Road
Minneapolis, Minnesota 55438

Printed in U.S.A.

Acknowledgments

I would like to thank The Salvation Army for permission to use the poem *A Dunce In Your School* by Flora Larrson, from *Just a Moment, Lord*. I am indebted to the writings of Watchman Nee, edited by Andrew Kinnear, published by Victory Press; and to my brother, Michael, who preserved the letters I wrote from Shanghai to Hong Kong.

Contents

Lesson One

In God's School

Far from seeking to avoid the world we need to see how privileged we are to have been placed there by God. 'As thou didst send me into the world, even so send I them into the world.' What a statement! The church is Jesus' successor, a divine settlement planted right here in the midst of Satan's territory.

WATCHMAN NEE in **Love Not the World**

There is a school of sorrow. There is a school of trial and persecution; and men who have not graduated in that school do not prove very good helpers for the churches.

JAMES HUDSON TAYLOR

THE FORLORN BENCHES of need, the sick women with their secrets, the watching men, the children sitting cautiously; one by one, stepping forward to whisper their problems, their faces and voices controlled, their deepest fears unspoken; and some leaving with fresh hope, their heads higher.

I was seventeen, nearing my birthday, and I was dreaming, as the young do, of my future; of being a doctor, dressing wounds, dispensing medicine, bringing solace, practising the art of healing.

'Tell me, where's the pain?'

To be a healer, enabled by God, in a communist country, my own beautiful country . . . could it be a possibility?

An ordinary Chinese girl following in the steps pioneered by Elizabeth Blackwell, the first woman doctor, who had overcome unbelievable hostility to qualify.

'Women doctors!' they had laughed at her, 'how about men mothers?'

'Unheard of . . . A woman doctor.'

She had made application to twenty-nine medical colleges in America, but here was I in Shanghai with a door wide open before me. Trying to control my pleasure I wrote that September day in 1953 to my brother, Michael, in Hong Kong.

Yesterday the newspaper published the examination results for the whole country, and I was overwhelmed to find that I was chosen according to my first wish and also the first college that I applied for, but I am a bit disappointed that I am asked to study for only the shorter, two-and-a-half-year course. If you enter into the proper course you have to learn all the specialised fields but in the shorter course I will concentrate on paediatrics. I can hardly imagine myself as a doctor in two and a half years. I am so young. How could I shoulder such responsibility? During the last few days you can imagine I have been rather restless waiting for the results. I had committed everything to God knowing he would guide me with his highest plan. Without this assurance I would have gone mad. I must say not many are selected to go to this very fine medical school because the standards of entry are so high. I cannot claim that I did well enough to deserve this. It truly passes my understanding, but I am sure you will be happy for me and so will father.

I do not know when I will move into the college but I will let you know. I need much prayer that my heart will be kept in humility.

Two weeks later I wrote that I would be registering at the college in three days' time.

The nation is paying all my expenses, except for some books which we have to buy ourselves and of course clothing. My needs will be modest compared with the last two months living in Shanghai. All the books are very expensive and I must decide whether to buy them for myself. It is convenient to have one's own books but on the other hand I will do without them if I can. It is frightening how much I have had to spend in Shanghai compared with living at home with mother.

Regarding my shorter course the government has assured us that as we are willing to accept this special course there will be opportunity for further refresher courses later. My prayer is that the Lord will strengthen me in the intensive studies so that I may be able to grasp all that is required of me. I trust you will not forget me in prayer. How is father's health? Please give him my love and ask him to forgive me for not writing to him.

'I dressed the wound,' wrote a wise surgeon, 'but God healed it.'

It was how I visualised my future. Missionary nurses and doctors had pioneered hospitals and clinics in China, training thousands of nurses and fine doctors, establishing the highest standards of practice and hygiene. Of thirteen medical colleges in 1930 eight were missionary institutions each underlining God and man working in harmony.

Following the communist revolution in 1948, the missionaries, including the doctors, were dismissed. For some it was a long trek home.

China was left with slightly more than twelve thousand doctors. Few of the four million Chinese who died each year from infectious and parasitic diseases had received professional treatment. There were households who never saw a doctor, child-bearing women who were not examined, children growing up unnecessarily handicapped.

Chairman Mao's worthy vision was of a new battalion of Chinese doctors, professionally qualified, scattered throughout China's four million square miles. A doctor within reach of everyone, however remote, whatever his income. His original plan was for western style medicine, with traditional Chinese practices, herbal medicines and acupuncture as extras.

I was to enter The First Medical College of Shanghai, originally built for training four hundred doctors, but now taking two thousand students.

My disappointment at being selected for the shorter course was genuine, but on the day I went to register at the college a miracle happened. I wrote:

I am so excited. They have changed me from the shorter course into the original full-term one. I cannot express my joy. I wonder why God is so extraordinarily good to me? This was a hope in my heart but since he had done so much for me I could not ask for more. Yet he knew my hidden thought and brought it to pass. I do not deserve this.

My curriculum would now include the usual subjects, as in every medical college, including anatomy, physiology, physics, chemistry, biochemistry, bacteriology, microbiology and zoology, plus the general clinical subjects with emphasis on the major in which one specialised.

I was to fulfil my ambition, learning to diagnose, to prescribe, to operate, to deliver babies, to remain unruffled in an emergency. Before my first lecture, my notebooks empty,

I pictured myself with stethoscope, pills, splints, bandages and bottles of medicine. But in the sharp sweetness of the dream there was some fear.

I was a Christian girl, the daughter of an exiled Chinese pastor who had angered the communists. Instead of losing all privileges, by a combination of God-ordained circumstances I was to be a medical student. I might have been in a labour camp, homeless, hungry, enclosed, with soldiers patrolling outside.

'Keep me true, God,' I prayed, thinking of those in this re-born nation who had renounced their faith in the face of dispossession, intimidation, violence. 'Make me worthy of this honour of bearing your name in college. Be my God, as you are father's God.'

Music had been my first love, my career-hope, but the regime had said medicine. God, I considered, would approve. Indeed, I believed that the wind of God, which blows whence it will, had brought me to Shanghai: that nothing happened by accident.

On registration I viewed the spotless lecture halls, laboratories, the enormous dining room, library and administrative office. Bricklayers, plasterers, carpenters, with disciplined unskilled labour, were completing dormitories and lecture rooms.

Shanghai had been sticky and uncomfortable, in contrast to my home in northern China, but now the days were cool and pleasant, the leaves turning colour and gently falling. My few possessions were packed in readiness: like my contemporaries I travelled light. I wrote again to Michael.

The college is in beautiful surroundings and is the original national medical college of Shanghai. It was founded in 1927. The dormitories are about five minutes' walk away, completely new, fourteen in a room with bunks. Of course I know nobody. I am moving in tomorrow and I have been assigned to specialise in paediatrics. Will you please pray that I may prepare myself not only for a medical career, but that these four years of training will one day become evidence of God's grace in my life?

I can never express how much he loves me. As I write I am made almost speechless by thinking of it. I have nothing and have done nothing to deserve such an endorsement of God's blessing. I need your prayers that I may not stumble. To be a doctor is something glorious humanly speaking, but I can already sense the subtle ways in which Satan will put pride in my heart.

May I not lose God for earthly gain, no matter how greatly I am tempted.

I put out the light. I would be the youngest girl in my year, a tiny statistic in the records of the new China. In the past, at home, I had been supported by my family and church; such bastions: but I could not remain a child. They had been my strength, but separated by thousands of miles I had to look directly to God.

I did not fully understand, but Mao's ambition was that privileged medical students, as they progressed with their studies, should swallow communism as patients swallowed medicine. He was relying on persuasion not force. 'When the wind blows the grass bends.'

They asked Daniel in the days of the Old Testament, 'Is your God, whom you serve, able to deliver you?' I suspected that, although a teenager, I was being transferred to a more adult grade in God's school. I was leaving the sheltered, junior establishment for a sterner place, where the adversary was formidable.

I did not seek a blaze of triumph but an opportunity quietly to prove God's sufficiency. 'For God alone,' said the Psalmist, 'my soul waits in silence, for my hope is from him. He only is my rock and my salvation, my fortress; I shall not be shaken. On God rests my deliverance and my honour; my mighty rock, my refuge is God.'

In the lecture room, the laboratory, the dormitories, the wards – God alone would be my salvation. Tomorrow, and the day after that, I would be baffled and beaten, if I did not lean on him.

Today, I look back at the vicissitudes of those years with thankfulness. I made mistakes, I had mishaps, I wept. When freedom seemed in jeopardy my sleep was disturbed by nightmares. For a year I was plagued constantly about my future. Where would I be tomorrow, next week? Would the family ever be reunited?

There was fun and laughter but little skylarking, and there came a bitter day when, after anguished hours of interrogation, I asked: 'God, is it not enough if I believe you in my heart and do not say so? If I deny your name would you not understand?'

I had been confined to a room for several days. Not caring what happened, disobeying instructions, I opened the door and ran into the recreation field. It was raining. Caution had gone. I think I was momentarily mad.

'God where are you?' I screamed in the night. 'Don't you care about me any more?' I barely noticed the rain.

He came swiftly.

'You know better than this,' God whispered. 'You have experienced me. Others might question but not you.'

A new dawn broke and I was soothed.

My friends have persuaded me to share these lessons from a Shanghai branch of God's school. I was spiritually frail, not a leader, or a strong person that people turned to for inspiration. I was a little Christian with a big God, in Watchman Nee's words I was 'in a divine settlement planted in the midst of Satan's territory'.

Prayer

I would take the events of my life as good and perfect gifts from thee; I would receive even the sorrows of my life as disguised gifts from thee. I would have my heart open at all times to receive – at morning, noon, and night; in spring, and summer, and winter. Whether thou comest to me in sunshine or in rain, I would take thee into my heart joyfully.
                                        George Matheson

Lesson Two

Confessing Him

No one can force a single soul, Christian (so-called) or heathen, to turn to Christ. All his followers have to do, all they can do, is to lift up Christ before the world, bring him into dingy corners and dark places of the earth where he is unknown, introduce him to strangers, talk about him to everybody, and live so closely with and in him that others may see that there really is such a person as Jesus, because some human being proves it by being like him.

Written by Betty Stam who died in her twenties, with her husband, at the hands of the communists.

SHANGHAI WAS MY home for the duration of medical training. The gateway to the Yangtse Lake Plains and the greatest seaport in China, it was over a century old, having been a fishing village in 1843.

In the north I had lived by the sea but never had I seen so many people, about six million. In style and outlook it was the most western of Chinese cities and until the revolution was an international city, a base for foreign traders. Because of the absence of good internal communications, and the reliance on international capital and trade, both industrial and commercial development in China had been largely in ports like Shanghai, Tientsin and Canton.

With modern administrative office blocks, busy factories, and a great pool of labour, it retained a measure of religious freedom long after the hinterland, but change was everywhere. Only the weather seemed to be beyond the influence of Mao.

In some spheres there was commendable progress. Food was better distributed; gambling, prostitution and stealing had dwindled. There was a new nationalism and patriotism among the young, although loyalty to the state was taking the place of the traditional loyalty to the family.

I was proud to be Chinese — likewise the nurse who had opened her home to me during the weeks until term began. Her father had preached in my father's church. She introduced me to her assembly in Nanyang Road although the pastor, Watchman Nee, was in prison. One of the most able Bible teachers, he would not be silenced or compromised.

We went on the single-decker tram to the Sunday services. My home congregation had decreased, but here I found nearly one thousand of God's people singing and praying, listening to Biblical exposition, clutching the freedom which might disappear. The fellowship was beautiful.

Outside the assembly, portraits of Mao were going up, on posters, painted on walls, reproduced on silk and in concrete. 'Hail Divine Caesar,' the Romans said, but never quite like this.

Inside the assembly, the God of Abraham, of Isaac and of Jacob, the God and Father of our Lord Jesus Christ remained the source and centre of worship. 'Hallelujah: for the Lord God omnipotent reigneth.'

As I sat in the service I relived my experience at the examination when I arrived in Shanghai. 'Are you still a Christian?' I was asked. It was not a casual question. There were no areas of privacy. The examiner bluntly suggested that after four years of 'liberation' I should have relinquished my old ideas about God.

'I intend to remain a Christian,' I said meekly.

'You need re-education,' he snapped, making a note on his pad. If he saw me in Watchman Nee's church that view would be reinforced for these people were known as Jesus-lovers.

I asked God a favour. 'It would mean much, dear Lord, if I could find one true Christian friend in college, with whom I could pray, share, confide about my family.'

God had said, 'Behold, I am with you.' I was a pastor's daughter, but I lacked confidence in God alone. I sought a friend, a girl of my own age.

On the morning term started I knelt to pray, in a flutter, with the girl whose hospitality I had enjoyed. She asked God to grant moral and physical strength and prosperity in my studies. She had summoned a tricycle, a rare luxury, for the journey to what had been the French sector, on the south side of the river on the outskirts of Shanghai, where the college adjoined a large hospital.

As we bumped along I reminded myself that my new life must start with a confession of my faith. Had not Jesus said, 'So everyone who acknowledges me before men, I also will acknowledge before my Father who is in Heaven; but whoever denies me before men, I also will deny before my Father who is in Heaven' (Matt. 32: 33)?

'Be circumspect,' Satan whispered, donning an angel's garment. 'If you must believe, be discreet. After all, Jesus said, "When you pray, close the door." Do this and your training will lead to open doors. Few will know your father was a pastor, that you played hymns in church. You're hundreds of miles from home. Build a new life.'

The temptation was not unattractive – temptation rarely is. It was both compelling and horrific. 'Get thee behind me, Satan.'

As we reached the entrance I saw I was not alone in my newness. There were five hundred other first-timers, with bedding, bowls and chopsticks. We entered the main door of the stone-built four-storey building, with its flat roof, noting where mail was collected, and seeing the maze of corridors leading to administrative offices and the private quarters of the professors.

The newcomers talked softly, while established students greeted each other with noisy pleasure, sharing experiences, letting off steam. Students in surgery, medicine, gynaecology and obstetrics, paediatrics, or public health. I was glad that I had been selected for paediatrics.

In the fourth year an old Chinese doctor, not professionally qualified but with the wisdom of centuries would take us for two hours a week in traditional Chinese medicine. He was consultant for the wing of the hospital occupied by older patients and those with rare diseases.

'Can you read Russian?' someone chirped. I shuddered. English books had been discarded in 1950, part of a purifying process, in favour of Russian and Chinese texts, but there were insufficient of these and thousands of handwritten stencils had to be produced in an office equipped for the task.

The extent of the college startled me. Leaving the main building, crossing the lovely campus grounds, with neat individual houses for professors and senior lecturers, I came to the road with the new dormitories. Behind these at the rear of the campus, were shaky wooden structures, where the baker lived and the tailor, a genuine craftsman, who excelled at patching and turning worn clothes inside out.

The heart of the college was the dining room, also used for major functions and lectures. Row upon row of square tables, seating eight, arranged with precision.

I joined a queue at one of about twenty stands where vegetables and meat were served. I was hungry. Meat was measured out, but rice was plentiful and I served myself.

I carried my food to a corner table. At home we said grace, whoever was present. Father's voice had boomed, 'Lord, we thank thee for the provision thou hast made for all our needs . . .' No one could mistake him. In our small home he used the same volume as in church. Sometimes during the Japanese occupation, food had been short, but not the grace. Now, surrounded by unbelievers, far from home, what should I do?

It was my first real question as a student, probing, frightening for a moment. 'Acknowledge Christ the first chance you have: the second will be tougher.' The words flashed across my mind. Here was my opportunity.

I must close my eyes and silently give thanks. With a quick, diffident glance, I bowed my head.

'I thank you Lord for all these days and for leading me so far. At last I am here. I thank you for this food. There may be no other Christian in this dining room, but if there is direct her or his eyes to look at me now.'

I hungered for God and for fellowship. I was treading the beaten track of aspiring feet down many centuries. I would not be submerged. With my faith in the open I would be happier, freer. An unworthy disciple, maybe, but never, I hoped, a secret disciple.

'May they all know that I am a believer.'

A girl was striding towards me as I opened my eyes. Her hair was long, in the style worn by believers, her eyes, her shining face, her confident step declared she was a Christian. She had seen me pray. Dashingly, she stretched out her hand, her face aglow.

'Dear sister in Christ,' she said, 'I welcome you to this college.'

Sweet, sweet words. Jesus said, 'Mary'. Like the woman at the tomb my heart overflowed.

She lifted her hand signalling across the dining hall. I looked in astonishment as eight or nine young men strode towards us, each, I was to find, a member of the college Christian fellowship. They had been looking for Christians to confess their faith in the simple act of thanksgiving.

'O God, how good you are to me. Let the world know I am yours.'

I asked him for one friend and my prayer was answered a hundredfold, for among the two thousand students there existed a Christian community which, while intensely loyal to China, did not think in Marxist terms. A Christian group which was a challenge to the thought-reformers, and indoctrinators, and ever active Youth League.

Shortly after I wrote to Michael:

I have been attending lectures for four days; it is very busy and I am under pressure; but of course I am now in college. For the basic studies we are together — chemistry, physics, biology, Russian, politics etc. God wonderfully led me to meet other Christians. I cannot describe. Maybe one day when he allows us to see each other I will share. We have fellowship between 6 p.m. and 7 p.m. after supper. I have already been so blessed. Among over two thousand students in the college there are one hundred Christians.

Every Friday there is leadership training for those totally committed to Christ. About twenty-five of us were there. Right now we are seeking to know how each one of us should be assigned to meet the need of the fellowship. Most probably for the final year I will be the pianist. We have one desire that God may be manifest through us as a group that represents the Body of Christ.

I have not found one Christian in my dormitory, but of course everybody is very quiet, not wanting to share too much about their personal lives. We come from different parts of China. To commit oneself can be very costly. I need extra grace, protection and especially discernment. Will you pray for me, particularly for this?

Prayer

> *How shall I thank thee for the grace,*
> *On me and all mankind bestowed?*
> *O that my every breath were praise!*
> *O that my heart were filled with God!*
> *My heart would then with love o'erflow,*
> *And all my life thy glory show.*
>
> Charles Wesley

Lesson Three

Pleasing Him

The triumph of communism brought the greatest reverse which Christianity had suffered in China for at least a century and a half. It threatened the very existence of the faith in that country. Ostensibly the communists granted religious liberty, but only in their sense of that term. They strove to eradicate from the churches all traces of what they deemed foreign imperialism. By the end of 1952 almost all missionaries, Roman Catholic and Protestant, had either voluntarily left or had been forcibly expelled. Most of the few who remained were either in prison or were confined to their homes and could not carry on normal activities. Not for nearly a hundred years had there been so few missionaries in China ... Church leaders and Christian constituencies were subjected to indoctrination in communist ideology.

KENNETH SCOTT LATOURETTE'S
A History of Christianity

FOR ME, IN the whole of Asia, there was no man like my father. A home, a church, an outing, a meal, came to life when he appeared. He could make a dull day rosy, a humdrum meal a feast, and wherever he went he appeared to fan a spark of faith into a flame.

His formal education started late, when he had almost despaired. At fourteen, he was ready to start a man's job, then was given the opportunity of a few months at a mission school. It was five days' walk from home, but he would have walked for a month. He was so apt a pupil that his mother secured a loan to keep him there. He qualified as a teacher and went to theological college, completing the course while supporting himself and his mother. After being an assistant lecturer, he had a year at Yenching University in Peking.

He married at thirty-three; of nine children, five died, leaving my two brothers, a younger sister, and myself. By western standards we were poor, but we were rich with music of our own making, with voice, trumpet and piano; with kindling stories, and the warm love on which families thrive.

Our world began to crumble when the communists came. The chilly winds stole into our home; the apprehension night and day, although there was nothing offensive in their early behaviour in our city. Mao had instructed, 'Wherever our comrades go, they must build good relations with the masses, be concerned for them and help them overcome their difficulties'.

They talked of a new democratic policy, of government in the hands of the people, of humanitarian concern. There were the famous Eight Points for Attention.

1. Speak politely.
2. Pay fairly for what you buy.

3. Return everything you borrow.
4. Pay for anything you damage.
5. Do not hit or swear at people.
6. Do not damage crops.
7. Do not take liberties with women.
8. Do not ill-treat captives.

Yet there was a fateful foreboding in the air. In 1950, two years after the People's Republic was proclaimed, they began to take an unhealthy interest in our church.

As a young man, father had raised the capital for it, supervised the building, lifting, carrying, sweating, as the foundations were dug and the walls rose. After the worship and prayers of several generations it was indeed the house of God to him.

His heart was pierced when Party members came to inspect it for their temporary use. There was misery in his eyes. It was for community purposes, they explained, suggesting this was his chance to show co-operation and goodwill. A communist organised meeting in his church? He was aghast.

He made conditions under which they might hold a district meeting. When they flagrantly broke the rules a confrontation took place. After sunset on January 2, 1951, to avoid arrest he left home, little knowing he would never return.

They brought ten charges against him, but in reality there was one — his rocklike faith. No coaxing, no pleading, no threat, would budge him. He loved nobly and unselfishly his home, his family, the familiar city, but even more the honour of Christ's name.

There were aspects of the revolution he admired. When Mao said, 'We should be modest and prudent, guard against arrogance and rashness, and serve the Chinese people heart and soul,' he could say Amen. His desire was not to be anti-communist but *for God*. It was all that mattered to him. His standards were absolute.

Father had a simple question which became a rule of life: 'Will it please God?'

'The only way I can please him is to do his will,' he would say. 'And to please him is my sole objective.'

With this question 'Will it please him?' big and small decisions, matters of tiny consequence, and of life and death, were set in the dimension of eternity. If pleasing God led to persecution he could say with Peter 'We must obey God rather than man' (Acts 5: 29).

Enoch, that giant of the Old Testament, was an example. 'By faith Enoch was taken up so that he should not see death; and he was not found, because God had taken him. Now before he was taken he was attested as having pleased God. And without faith it is impossible to please him' (Heb. 11: 5, 6).

Until the communists came, even in the Japanese occupation pleasing God seemed relatively uncomplicated; like travelling along a straight road and not being distracted by the signposts. Keeping one's eye on the goal. The road was never to be as straight again, and for thousands it was to go through the valley of death.

The heart-breaking choice was now between pleasing God and pleasing the state. In Chinese fashion he looked in vain for a middle path. There was none. He was in a society which feared his function, and wished to obliterate his God. 'Our God is none other than the masses of the Chinese people,' Mao said.

'No matter what, I will obey God,' father said. 'I choose rather to share ill-treatment with the people of God than to enjoy the pleasure of sin; to consider abuse suffered for Christ greater wealth than the treasures of Egypt. I will be judged as a reactionary and I regret that, but God's judgment is more to be feared.'

He recalled Abel, a son of Adam and Eve, and brother of Cain. Abel was a shepherd and his brother a tiller of the ground. His sacrifice excelled Cain's and pleased God. The writer to the Hebrews gives 'faith' as the reason. The two brothers knew that God regarded their offering differently: Abel had pleased the Almighty, Cain had displeased him.

Father saw that pleasing God does not lead to an easy life: Abel was slain. 'By faith Abel offered to God a more acceptable sacrifice than Cain, through which he received approval as righteous, God bearing witness by accepting his gifts; he died, but through his faith he is still speaking.'

'Abel pleased God,' father would explain, 'because he

treated God's inspiration and revelation seriously. Cain followed his own thinking and so, although he offered what the earth produced, he displeased God.'

We discussed this in our college fellowship between lectures and decided there were four questions we should ask ourselves at every crossroad.

Is it glorifying to God? Paul told the Corinthian church: 'So, whether you eat or drink, or whatever you do, do all to the glory of God.'

Is it edifying to others? Paul admonished: 'Let no one seek his own good, but the good of his neighbour.'

Is it helpful — expedient? 'All things are lawful, but not all things are helpful. All things are lawful, but not all things build up.'

Does it enslave? 'All things are lawful,' said Paul, but adds, 'I will not be enslaved by anything.' It may be legal to buy it, possess it, use it, but for the sake of Christ I will not. Never, no matter how beautiful its possession, how pleasurable the moment.

I told the fellowship of father's cousin, an intelligent, educated woman, formerly head of a women's Bible seminary in Shanghai, who had a similar philosophy to father. After much deliberation she would go to a store to choose material for a new garment. To get her there was a miracle. At the moment of decision she would ask, 'Am I pleasing God in this?'

In the choice of clothes, in the style of hair, in fixing a time-table, she quietly meditated. It often meant no purchase. God had other uses for her time and money.

'Whate'er is good to wish, ask that of heaven,' wrote Hartley Coleridge, 'Though it be what thou canst not hope to see; But if for any wish thou dar'st not pray, Then pray to God to cast that wish away.'

The Lord Jesus, Scripture tells us, did not please himself. This, as one old preacher put it, involved the Master in an inward war, for pleasing God meant displeasing his family, the leaders of his nation, the venerable fathers of the Jewish faith; it meant desertion by his friends and calumny from his enemies; it meant being thought a traitor by his nation.

'Am I now,' asked Paul, 'seeking the favour of men, or of God? Or am I trying to please men? If I were still pleasing men, I should not be a servant of Christ. For I would have you know, brethren, that the Gospel which was preached by me is not man's Gospel' (Gal. I: 10, 11).

In God's school I speedily found that pleasing God meant sometimes displeasing those around me, for the mind that is set on the flesh, as Paul succinctly puts it, is hostile to God.

Prayer

May I only do those things which please thee.

Lesson Four

Communing with Him

Always a sleepy head, it was wonderful to me to be awakened each morning, as I was, and in the quiet of that still hour, Christ became so real to me that often I felt I could have touched him, if I but put out my hand. I was learning what Dr. A. W. Tozer calls 'the awareness of his presence'. It satisfied me as nothing on earth had done. It filled me with a joy of communion that is inexpressible.

ISOBEL KUHN in **By Searching**

WHATEVER THEIR NATIONALITY or background, throughout China Christians faced criticism, persuasion and re-education. Geoffrey Bull, a missionary, who was for three years a prisoner of the communists, told in *When Iron Gates Yield* how he was caught up in the nationwide campaign for the suppression of counter-revolutionaries. In Chungking, four thousand arrests were made in one night, filling the prisons and flooding detention centres. In a reign of terror father exposed son, and son exposed father, mothers and daughters exposed husbands and brothers.

A fellow-prisoner told Mr. Bull that he had attended one mass meeting where sixty-eight people were massacred before a mob who demanded that such enemies of the people be swept from the earth. For Geoffrey Bull himself, day after day, the threat of execution continued.

He demonstrated outstanding courage. If he lived, or if he died, he prayed that it would be with the name of Jesus on his lips. With no Bible, and no fellowship, with his mind battered and fatigued, often in a dark cell, communion with God sustained his faith. Strength received through ordered meditation on the Scriptures was, he believed, what brought him through.

I had my Bible. I had other Christians near me. I was a student and not a prisoner. Yet I was to find how indispensable was this personal communion. Without it my faith would have disappeared in the tidal wave sweeping China.

'We are a nation of millions and we are united as a single man,' the Communists declared. But my allegiance was to Christ — not to China's past, not the revolution, not capitalism, but to the Saviour.

If only our family were reunited. Father and Michael were struggling for an existence in Hong Kong, Martin was planning a career, while mother and my sister Ruby were at home in the north. I had prayed that they might move to Shanghai. There was greater freedom, and it was nearer Hong Kong.

In November, 1953 mother and Ruby made the journey, about a thousand miles. It meant leaving home and personal property behind, but that was of no consequence. I told Michael:

> I am so happy. This very afternoon I went to meet mother and Ruby. I am so thankful to the Lord that after a long journey mother was not sick. They had to change trains many times and were delayed for eight hours. I took them straight to the sister with whom they are to stay. Her place is very small but she is extremely kind. I had to take them to register with the local police. There was no problem. I was rather apprehensive about this and on the journey prayed hard, but how wonderful that God helped us. He does not withhold any good thing. He is our God. I cannot help but recall the way he leads.
>
> Our life is busy. Apart from lectures and the fellowship meetings, I spend all my time studying and the day is not long enough. On Monday, Tuesday and Thursday we have prayer meetings. Wednesday we have a fellowship and sharing meeting. Friday is Bible study. This is in addition to the early morning prayer. I do want you to pray particularly for the coming evangelistic meetings planned by our fellowship. Humanly speaking we are trying to do the impossible. If we depend on ourselves nothing can be done, but we know there is a need to share the Gospel with our fellow students. We have not been forbidden although the arrangements are known.

Our early morning prayer meetings were held on the flat roof of the pharmacy, after our private prayer, twenty or twenty-five, arriving soon after 6 a.m. It was cold and damp in the winter, but if we were a windswept group we had not been called to ease or leisure. There is, said Hudson Taylor, both blessed prosperity and blessed adversity. Kneeling on our cushions, on frosty mornings, the freedom to pray together was a blessed prosperity, but for how long no one knew.

'Brothers and sisters, I request your prayer this morning,' one whispered. 'My faith is ebbing.'

Someone confessed, 'Yesterday I was defeated. I failed to make a stand. I'm miserable. Remember me.'

'I would like you to pray for my family,' I asked.

Our silent prayers ascended, and in the drawing near to God, we came closer to each other.

On Christmas Day, 1953 I wrote:

As today is Christmas I send you greetings. Here there are few Christmas celebrations compared with earlier years, but there are more in Shanghai than in the country districts. I was refreshed to see a Christmas tree outside a church. Yesterday we moved to a new dormitory. Seven of us are in the same room. I am the only Christian, but I want to share with you that a week ago one of my former room-mates finally had the courage to admit to me that she was a Christian. This is because she saw me reading the Bible and praying. In fact she sleeps on the top of my bunk. Of course the joy was tremendous for me, but I was reminded of my shortcomings.

Why did not my life give her the courage and confidence that she could share this with me from the beginning? If I had been more loving?

It is impossible to ask everybody whether they are Christians or not. I told you we had five in my class, but now we have discovered two more. We have begun our class fellowship together with those who are majoring in gynaecology.

At the new year our Christian fellowship will have three days of evangelistic meetings for college students. All of us will do our best to bring non-Christians. I don't know what to expect but I'm praying that my life will not hinder anyone from coming to Christ. I increasingly re-alise how important this is.

We have started our Bible study on the book of Ephesians.

This letter, like others, was written on American Red Cross notepaper, which I had bought on a street-stall. I saw a little of Shanghai at weekends; gay stalls, shops and restaurants catering for one of the most densely populated areas of the world. Cyclists and pedestrians mingled on the streets, but usually there was little time for sight-seeing.

In the last three weeks I have become so tired with the intensive study, and everything new, that I am finding it difficult to wake as early as I should. Will you pray that I may wake up at 5.30? This is hard but I must because it is only through prayer and Bible reading that I can draw strength for the day. I need at least half an hour to three quarters for this, judging the load I carry every day. We do exercises at 6.45, and at 7.30 are in the lecture rooms. I praise God that every morning he fails me not. This must be my secret, yet I know I am so weak.

The Christians in my class have expressed the desire to have fellowship together apart from, but in addition to, the larger fellowship for the whole college. We must meet. The only possible time is the break in mid-morning, when there is ten minutes for us to share. May God direct us.

I know you are not forgetting the brothers and sisters at home. Whenever I think of them I see them as fellow-runners in the race. We may start together, but we are not competing like the other athletes. We are to encourage one another. It is not easy, in fact harder and harder, and especially when trials come from those who were once with us in the faith. Their cross is heavier than mine, but I praise God that they established a foundation for my life. God knows how easily I fall, which is why he moved me here from there.

To go to sleep talking with God, to awake communing with him, and to stay in touch throughout the day, was our target, to be channels of unseen resources. If we started with a sense of the holy, accepting that absolute power is with God, that we were utterly dependent on him, we would not succumb. There were practical problems.

The days become so much darker. It is no longer possible for me to read my Bible on my bunk early in the morning. The light outside my window is out of order. I cannot switch on the interior light because it would wake the others. I very quietly get off my bunk and, praise God, I have found a corner under a dim light in the corridor where I can just manage to read. Of course once the bell rings for getting up one can switch on the light, but you can imagine the confusion then. When it is not raining or snowing I can sit outside and the air is very fresh. I am writing this letter out of doors on this spot.

Like Isobel Kuhn, in the quiet of the still early morning hour, I found the joy of communion that is inexpressible. Christ became so real that I too felt I could have touched him, if I but put out my hand.

Prayer

> *O God, thou art my God; early will I seek thee:*
> *For thy loving kindness is better than life,*
> *My lips shall praise thee.*
> *My soul shall be satisfied as with marrow and fatness;*
> *And my mouth shall praise thee with joyful lips;*
> *When I remember thee upon my bed,*
> *And meditate on thee in the night watches,*
> *For thou hast been my help,*
> *And in the shadow of thy wings will I rejoice.*
> *My soul followeth hard after thee:*
> *Thy right hand upholdeth me.*
>
> Psalm 63: 1, 3, 5–8

Lesson Five

Broken Before Him

It was not Jacob who wrestled, but God who came and wrestled with him, to bring about his utter surrender. The object of wrestling is to force a man down until he is unable to move, so that he yields to the victor. Yet of God it is said that even here, 'He prevailed not'. Jacob possessed tremendous natural strength. Most of us know all too well what this means. We can do so well ourselves; we employ all sorts of natural skills for our self-protection ... One day we must acknowledge defeat, confessing that we know nothing at all and can do nothing at all.

WATCHMAN NEE in **Changed into His Likeness**

MY LOVING BROTHER, Michael, sent small parcels from Hong Kong. Their arrival gave me immense pleasure. They contained few extravagances but sometimes a messenger from Heaven. One was a Chinese edition of *The Calvary Road* by Roy Hession. This little book, now available in forty languages, was published in 1950. Neither the author nor the publishers saw it as a best-seller, but God had a unique role for it. It was itself the product of a revival when God began to manifest himself in the infant church in Ruanda, East Africa. The revival spread to Uganda, Kenya, and Tanzania, with thousands, missionaries among them, finding a fresh quality of life.

In April 1947 Roy Hession, in a state of spiritual need, invited to a convention he was organising in Britain several missionaries from East Africa. As he listened, he discovered that he was the neediest person in the conference.

As my wife and others humbled themselves before God and experienced the cleansing of the blood of Jesus, I found myself left somewhat high and dry — dry just because I was so high. I was humbled by the simplicity of what I had to do to be revived and filled with the Spirit.

What he learned at that convention and in the following months was published mostly as articles, and later gathered together in *The Calvary Road*.

Now, in a language I could understand, it found its way to Shanghai. It had gripped Michael and he knew its message would challenge me. The necessity of being broken before God was its recurring theme, broken at the cross of Christ, as indeed Christ was broken for us.

Lord, bend that proud and stiffnecked I,
Help me to bow the head and die;

Beholding him on Calvary,
Who bowed his head for me.

I wrote to Michael:

> I want to thank you for sending me the books. I have been reading *The Calvary Road*. It is a great help. First of all it made me realise I had not been broken before him. And without that his power cannot be released through me. I have been praying for myself that I may have this willingness to accept his hand. I have now come to chapter eight. I cannot read very fast because I have to meditate and apply almost everything to my life. I would appreciate your sending more good books!

There were ideas which were new to me. I began to receive a fresh understanding of the blood of Christ, and of the part it must play before we can 'walk in the light, as he is in the light'. Walking in the light, I read, is simply walking with Jesus. Therefore there need be no bondage about it. But it meant having a new openness with the brethren as well as with God. And the purpose of 'walking in the light' was that we might 'have fellowship one with another'. Was I walking in the light? Was I open and honest before God and other believers? Was his victorious life filling me and overflowing to others? Was I calling sin, sin (my sin, not the other person's)?

As I read on there came another challenge. 'Nothing is clearer from the New Testament than that the Lord Jesus expects us to take the low position of servants.' A medical student a servant? He 'counted it not a prize to be on equality with God, but emptied himself, taking the form of a servant'. This servanthood was to express itself in service to our fellows. 'We preach not ourselves,' said Paul, 'but Christ Jesus our Lord; and ourselves your servants for Jesus' sake.' This was the path of the cross. What did I know of this humbling, this brokenness? This way down, that was the only way up? Was I willing for the light of God to go through every part of my life and into every part of my relationship?

I shared *The Calvary Road* with other Christians, as one might the discovery of treasure, although as Roy Hession said, this was no new, astounding doctrine. Rather, it was a life to live day by day in whatever circumstances God had put us. To each student it spoke differently, but it resulted in a united cry that God might break us.

I had been experiencing some spiritual depression. I was irritated by a lovely girl whose exuberance found expression in exclamations like, 'Isn't Jesus wonderful!' In father's church we had loved God but been more restrained. Her sincerity was apparent but I found her disturbing.

Dwelling on father's experience was making me moody and withdrawn. In despair I was believing but not loving. I was troubled for mother and her health. 'Isn't Jesus wonderful!' caused a sad reaction. How I needed to be broken.

Later this same girl, reflecting the beauty of Christ, was used to challenge me. Twice she rebuked me for not trusting God. It was a galling experience. The day came when I rejoiced in exclamations of delight in God. In the meantime I wrote to Hong Kong:

I must share with you that I do not understand why or what God wants me to learn, but I have become very discouraged and the peace within my heart has been disturbed. I know in him there should be no disappointment and the promises in him are yea and amen. In him there is peace, life and joy, but I need to experience this afresh and claim these promises. My own discouragement comes from Satan. I know he is very fierce, never giving up his attack on the children of God. The more we seek to identify with God the greater his activity. Pray that I may learn to take his attacks positively, recognising that these should drive me nearer to the Lord.

I am a bit confused. To know something theoretically is one thing but to know it experimentally is harder. Does this mean that throughout the Christian life I shall continue to be in conflict? I don't want to hide this from you but I am depressed and my depression shows itself in an increasing reluctance to have fellowship with other Christians. I find myself rather alone. Every morning I pray and read the Bible on the roof top, sometimes for one and a half hours, then I go to breakfast and lectures. Is there something wrong with me, or does God take us aside at times and teach us the lessons that we need to learn alone? But I am unhappy because the Christian fellowship should mean everything to me. These are the members of the same body and I have no doubt they are praying for me, and are worried for me. In future there might come a day when I can have no fellowship with anyone, when I shall have to stand alone, but while I can have fellowship why am I like this?

It may be that I am just too busy. Every day there is a twenty-four-hour programme. We spend more than seven hours in lectures and laboratory work and then I need almost five hours to revise. We have one hour of physical training which is to fit us to learn to defend our nation. My classmates, knowing I am a northerner, expect me to be physically stronger. Well, it is helpful to have the running and physical training. I miss my piano practice but I thank God I have now found a home where I can go and practise. In my limited time I aim to practise three hours a week. I don't have a teacher, but I will be satisfied if I can keep up what I have mastered. It also helps that I can return at the weekend to see mother and Ruby for half a day. In this time I teach Ruby the piano.

In April, 1954, at half-term, the Christian fellowship arranged a day of meetings. I missed the morning session having to go into Shanghai in a search for medicine for mother. When I returned in the afternoon the theme was the need for the openness and honesty before God of which I had been reading in *The Calvary Road*. I wrote to Michael:

Our leader suggests that we should all be absolutely open with each other, hiding nothing. Strangely enough as we opened up to each other I found what we all shared was our own weaknesses. Remember I told you I was so depressed. The letters from the north tell how the brothers and sisters there are also low spiritually. We were reminded of 2 Corinthians 4: 8: 'Afflicted in every way, but not crushed; perplexed, but not driven to despair; persecuted, but not forsaken; struck down, but not destroyed; always carrying in the body the death of Jesus, so that the life of Jesus may also be manifested in our bodies.'

We are all struck down. How strange after the revival we had in the beginning of this year when we saw such tremendous blessing in our evangelistic meetings. I think it is not by chance that we are like this, but that God would want us to go through such a valley to realise that we cannot depend on our own strength and maintain the spiritual level. In this meeting today God received the glory. He reminded us that we should forget the past and daily trust for fresh strength. We must learn to number our days. When days are gone they are gone. One brother reminded us that when Elijah was depressed the angel of God ministered unto him and said, 'Get up and eat', because he still had far to go. On this road to Calvary we have a cross. We have not been compelled to carry it, but of our own willingness take it. It is heavy going, but there is no return. Yet when we go ahead we find there is also sweetness.

The doctor says mother has hypertension, heart disease and asthma. I am upset because I cannot get her the medicine she needs. We are still applying for permission for mother and Ruby to join you, but perhaps we should concentrate only on mother as she is elderly and sick.

In a spirit of brokenness our fellowship cried, 'God have mercy on us.' Sin, as Roy Hession had suggested, was what we had in common with everyone else, and we found at the feet of Jesus, where sin is cleansed, the only place where we could be one.

We were quickened by the story of the saintly African who told a congregation how as he climbed a hill to a service he heard steps behind him. He turned and saw a man carrying a heavy load on his back up the hill. Full of sympathy he spoke to him. Then he saw that his hands were scarred. It was the Lord Jesus. 'Lord,' he said, 'are you carrying the world's sin up the hill?' 'No,' said Jesus, 'not the world's, just yours.'

Prayer

Lord, I acknowledge defeat. I confess that I know nothing at all and can do nothing at all. Bring me to the place of utter surrender, where I yield to you as victor.

Lesson Six

He Makes no Mistakes

Choose for us, God, nor let our weak preferring
Cheat us of good thou hast for us designed:
Choose for us, God;
Thy wisdom is unerring.
And we are fools and blind.

OUR CHINESE PROFESSORS, primarily graduates of western universities, had inherited the highest traditions and standards of professional behaviour. They had solemnly pledged themselves to the service of humanity; to practise their profession with conscience and dignity; to respect the secrets confided to them; to make the health of their patients their first consideration, and to maintain the utmost respect for human life from the time of conception.

They did not consider us as communists, Buddhists or Christians, but as entrants to a profession where in the words of Dr. P. T. Regester, 'one may well find oneself dying of overwork but never of boredom'. Some had been at the college since before 'liberation', and their concern was more with glands, intestines, gall-bladders, blood-cells, arteries and veins, than with the revolution, but they were not able to be aloof from it.

We had a medical and an administrative head, the former a medical consultant to Mao. The head of paediatrics was a lady, her husband a professor in surgery. They were American-trained. As in many western colleges we had an associate professor, lecturer and associate lecturer in each department, but saw little of them outside classes.

I was fairly competent in my studies, and there were sudden bursts of sunlight, moments of achievement. I accepted Mao's four health principles: health care must serve the common people; priority must be given to *preventing* disease; western and traditional medicine must be integrated; health campaigns must be co-ordinated with other mass campaigns.

I was absorbed by my studies. Only in the last century had there been a place for women in medical colleges. Elizabeth Blackwell believed women were in a unique position to serve the needs of female patients. She graduated in 1849 and was placed on the British Medical Register ten years later. In the next twelve years only one other woman's name was added. The opposition came not only from men. Florence Nightingale disapproved.

'There is no practical work outside domestic life,' said Dr. Blackwell, 'so eminently suited to their noble aspirations as the legitimate study and practice of medicine.'

Now on the other side of the world Mao was fulfilling her vision. Among poor peasants, women had always done their share of manual work, but new doors were opening with equal pay for equal work. 'China's women are a vast reserve of labour power,' said Mao. 'This reserve should be tapped in the struggle to build up a great socialist country.'

Party members sought to wash Chinese minds of the old ideas, filling them with new doctrines. A Catholic priest, Robert Greene, described a typical village scene which he witnessed at this period. The indoctrinator gathered the villagers together, then shouted out a question. The children repeated the words in sing-song fashion.

'Who is the great liberator of China?'

'The great liberator is our leader, Mao Tse-tung.'

'What country is the great enemy of our people?'

'The imperialist country of America.'

'Within our country who are the oppressors of our people?'

'The landlords and capitalists.'

'Why are our people poor and ill-fed?'

'Because of the landlords, who must be abolished.'

In a similar atmosphere of feverish frenzy, we were asked: 'Did you ever see the Lord of heaven? 'Did you ever see a spirit?'

In February 1954 Christian unions in senior high schools and colleges met together in Shanghai. There were 1,500 students and visitors at the services which went on from 8 a.m. to 5 p.m., in the Assembly Hall in Nanyang Road.

The evangelical churches in Shanghai, hearing that religious liberty had vanished in vast areas of China, and sensing that time was fast running out in the cities, also held evangelistic services. Hundreds confessed Christ as Saviour. In my home city there was a brief period of freedom, when the students held a conference. I informed Michael:

The whole of our four-day conference was fine. In the morning it was devotional, in the afternoon fellowship and prayer, in groups, or together as a whole. All the devotional talks were geared to the theme 'Lord, you have the word of eternal life. To whom shall we go?' This is the way to the cross. Why should we follow the Lord? What price must we be willing to pay? The first thing I learned was never to give room to Satan. All of us know attacks from him. I also learned that to be a Christian is an inner life and not just outward confession. Even in the circumstances we are now in, it is possible to concentrate on the outward and neglect the inner life. At the final open testimony time there was a brother from your old university. He told how he had left the Lord completely. He did not have anything to do with other Christians in the fellowship, which is probably why I didn't know him, but the love of God turned him back in the last six months. All of us were much blessed by him. His testimony reminded us of the immeasurable love of God, and, on the other hand, how terrible it is to fall into the hand of the Lord who is a consuming fire.

I asked God to help me not to judge others. When they are weak I want to share their weakness; when they are strong I want to share their strength. All the expenses were given by the students. Every day all of us, 1,500, had lunch there, and every day the Lord met our financial needs with something over. Mother and Ruby have applied for permission to go to Hong Kong, but this has not yet been granted.

In this new term we have anatomy, biochemistry, etc. I have passed my first examinations, although I did not spend as much time as I should to prepare but God has helped me. I constantly have a conflict: I ought to do my study well, but yet I should not make an idol of it that will take God's place. I treat my training and my study here as part of my spiritual training.

Gradually, I began to think and act like a medical student. I learned a fascinating vocabulary. I began to observe, to note the features, the eyes, the hands, the condition of the hair, tiny pointers to health or sickness. Embarrassment among us disappeared when certain topics were introduced by our professors. We talked with clinical detachment, in a frank manner, on topics which do not arise in mixed company.

As I discovered the extraordinary knowledge and wisdom of the professors my admiration grew, particularly as I travelled at a snail's pace. In June 1954 I wrote:

It is now almost the end of the first year. You will remember how timid I was and could never imagine myself taking a medical course. I don't mind hard work but the practical work of anatomy on dead bodies seemed too much. This I dreaded. Some young men in our class enjoyed teasing me. But I confess I am much better now. I have already done quite a bit, some of it when all the other students had left the room. I found myself so immersed in my work that once I did not realise I was alone with twelve corpses. I wanted to know exactly how the arteries carry blood and I became more and more fascinated. We only expose the part of the body we are studying while the rest of the body is covered. I jump for joy when I find a particular nerve. Three of us share a body!

Many say this subject is difficult but I am amazed by the minute, by the very fine handiwork of God who made us. And yet this great Creator is also our God who directs the tiniest features of our life.

The study of the human body, with its intricate living organisms, strengthened my faith in God. After a systematic study of bacteria I told Michael:

During my practical work for bacteriology we had to use the microscope a great deal and our eyes became strained because we were not used to it. I asked myself why God did not give us eyes to see these things without this instrument. But on reflection wouldn't it be horrible if we did have eyes which were able to see the living creatures moving about in the food we eat, in the air we breathe, in the things we touch? God makes no mistakes.

Did I really believe that last sentence, 'God makes no

mistakes'? In creation: no mistakes? Since time began: no mistakes? In permitting my family to be split up: no mistakes? In bringing me to Shanghai: no mistakes?

Indeed I did. Man erred, but God never.

Yet how often I wanted God to do my will, believing in his love, more than in his wisdom. But he alone knew what was good for me, with his infinite wisdom, infinite power.

I returned to the theme when Michael wrote to share an acute problem. In his trouble, where was God? I replied:

I know exactly how you feel, your burdens, your difficulties, but God understands. He will not forsake you. I pray that the Lord will deliver you out of this trouble and that joy from above will fill your heart . . . We are still earth-bound and there are things that drag our feet . . . But God never makes mistakes.

What a lesson to learn in God's school. If I knew his goal, if I saw his objective, I would not question. What a wretched mess I made when I tried to take control from him, to make my own destiny.

Prayer

O Lord, thou knowest what is best for us. Let this or that be done, as thou shalt please. Give what thou wilt, and how much thou wilt, and when thou wilt. Deal with me as thou thinkest good, and as best pleaseth thee. Set me where thou wilt, and deal with me in all things just as thou wilt. Behold, I am thy servant, prepared for all things; for I desire not to live unto myself, but unto thee; and oh, that I could do it worthily and perfectly. Amen.

Thomas à Kempis

Lesson Seven

Above an Ordinary Offering

How do we choose in life? What principles govern our actions? Most of us need to put into practice far more fully the principle of the cross, which is one of daily death to self and self-gratification. How often we choose the easier of two paths and therefore sometimes miss God's best for us. The harder path has the sharp pain of the cross in it, but also the glory of Easter morning.

Sacrifice by HOWARD GUINNESS

It is an easy thing to sing, 'I all on earth forsake'. It is not very difficult to think, and honestly though ignorantly say, 'I give up all to thee and for thee'. But God sometimes teaches one that that little word 'all' is terribly comprehensive.

JAMES HUDSON TAYLOR

'IN AN UNUSUAL time the Lord has unusual requests. He has asked me to offer myself above an ordinary offering.' The words are not those of a venerable saint in the Middle Ages, but of Sung Ling, a young woman writing from a labour camp in China.

I met this lovely Christian girl, who sought only the Lord's embrace, in Shanghai in 1955. She was twenty-seven, a lecturer in the Bible seminary, which was threatened with closure. How had it survived so long? The tutors and few students who remained accepted the crisis could not be long delayed, but none guessed how great an offering God was going to ask of Sung Ling.

She, with her colleagues, lived by faith, looking to God to provide their daily food.

I first met her in a spacious first-floor room, sparsely furnished, at the seminary. A prayer meeting had been arranged and the room was comfortably filled with staff and students. Little suspecting how significant my meeting with her would prove in future years,* I shyly accompanied another medical student. She greeted me with an infectious smile.

'Sister Wang, will you pray for me?' she asked when we were alone.

It was a modest enough request, but she was so mature, so capable, that I was numbed by it. I coveted her prayers. I was seven years younger in age, and decades in the spiritual life. I had no indication of the peril she was in.

Over several months a gentle bond of love grew between us. If I had guessed what the future held I would have clung to her; but I did not know. A kindly God has veiled the future from our sight. Because she was my senior I let her take the initiative, and she invariably suggested, not

* See *Stephen the Chinese Pastor*.

refreshments and a gossip, but a Bible reading together in her room.

Occasionally, as a special privilege, I was able to spend a day at the seminary. What fragrant hours they were. The staff gladly shared their food but one day I discovered the pantry was nearly bare.

We were all hard up, although for the first year of my college life my food was provided free. Michael sent gifts from Hong Kong and Martin, who was still in north China, was generous to me. There was always pressure, however, to use part of any gift towards buying government bonds. The balance provided writing materials, books, postage, my fares to church and a contribution for the offertory.

If my purse was empty I did not go to church. I hated to explain why, but I had to lean harder on God. I was challenged by the Lord to give, and sometimes to give all, for example when a Christian sister sought the fare to visit her mother in hospital in a distant province. I prayed with her in the storeroom. As I prayed an inner voice whispered, 'It sounds well for you to say you love this sister, but you have the answer to her prayer in your own pocket. If your mother was ill, and you had no money, wouldn't you be thankful for assistance?'

God was granting me the privilege of answering my own prayer.

I had eight dollars. I wrapped them in paper, and placed them under her pillow with her Bible. It meant remaining in college that weekend, but I was not gloomy. The misery descended when I did not heed God's voice.

When I discovered the critical situation at the seminary I looked in my purse. Instead of taking the normal amount for the offertory I gave everything except the return fare to college. I was only to fully understand how little this was when, years later, I saw the measure of Sung Ling's offering.

Her interrogators judged her narrow, stubborn, wilful, and she was sentenced to imprisonment and despatched to north-west China, where she suffered prolonged ill-health. Infrequent letters told of days when she was semi-conscious, with painful swellings in her spine. When she was judged fit she was employed in a factory.

In 1960 when I came to England I was invited to the Chinese church in London. Its pastor and founder was Sung

Ling's father, Stephen Wang. He was an exile from China and had not seen her for more than ten years. I shared every precious memory. His prayer was that she might be released to receive specialist medical treatment to save her life. He lovingly kept a handful of letters which he read and re-read. She wrote:

In an unusual time the Lord has unusual requests. He has asked me to offer myself above an ordinary offering. If I don't have no peace. Only when I say 'Yes' can I rest in him, and draw strength to go on where he wants me to go to the very end ... In the biography of Madame Guyon the last page has the hymn that she wrote when she was in prison. I have learned to sing this in the last two years, especially in the recent days of my complete offering to God. I have much joy and courage. I can fully understand how Paul and Silas sang together in prison.

For years there has been no authoritative word, and it is not known if she was ever released, or if she is alive. Others of our number echoed her declaration of complete surrender.

Trainee doctors in their fourth year, the future stretched before them, speculated about their first appointment. Each on graduation was invited to state a preference. It was understandable to name a town or city with medical and research facilities, a hospital and good accommodation, although the final choice was taken by the administrators in closed session.

Our fellowship debated the factors which should govern the choice of a Christian doctor. Shanghai, and two or three other major cities, had greater freedom for worship than country districts, but for how long? They also had advanced medical facilities.

'We should go to lonely, isolated regions, where the church is weakest,' one brother suggested.

'But the cities are the centres of influence,' someone ventured.

The fellowship named small towns and districts where the Gospel had barely penetrated.

A letter was read from a bright young doctor, a graduate

for whom we prayed. He pleaded for pioneers, 'to go beyond the ranges'.

We recalled the graduate who was the only doctor in a district of thirty-five square miles, with a horse for transport. His facilities were abysmally primitive.

'We must not be shamed by the communists,' a brother said.

In speeches and writing they were being urged by Mao to 'be the most far-sighted, the most self-sacrificing, the most resolute . . . It will take several decades to make China prosperous. Even then we will still have to observe the principle of diligence and frugality.'

Christians were never sent to an appointment together. The scattering of believers was intended to weaken the church, but it proved God's way of scattering the seed of the Gospel in spots where missionaries had made little impact.

Forgetting cosy dreams of a practice, with a hospital and laboratories on the doorstep, we prepared ourselves for a tough, disciplined life, in Sung Ling's words, 'above an ordinary offering'.

Like soldiers in training for an offensive we ate more frugally, omitting the surplus calories, to trim ourselves. We cut down on our sleep. We did not sacrifice our health, but aimed to be in the peak of fitness.

For me this was heady stuff. There were selfish, worldly ambitions not yet conquered.

'Every student who calls himself a Christian,' wrote Mildred Cable, a distinguished China missionary, 'is in duty bound to come directly to his Master for designation, and he must come with an open mind, a yielded will, and the words, not only on his lips but in his heart "for any manner of service I am wholly at thy command".'

Even to languish in a labour camp in north-west China with tuberculosis of the spine? Surely, God wanted Sung Ling to be free, to be well. 'In an unusual time,' she said, 'the Lord has unusual requests.'

Prayer

Lord, I do not first offer myself for Christian work, but to do your will, by your grace to be and to do whatever you may ask, wherever that may be. Amen.

Lesson Eight

Practising the Presence of God

The more disciplined we are in our set times of devotion, the more easy it will become to live the rest of our time in the presence of God.

JOHN R. W. STOTT

BROTHER LAWRENCE WAS a member of a lay community of Carmelites in Paris, where he was in charge of the kitchen. A hospital kitchen at that. His book *The Practice of the Presence of God,* first published in 1692, was sent to me by Michael. In his job as cook, Brother Lawrence learned to practise the presence of God until he came to the place 'wherein it would be as difficult for me not to think of God as it was at first to accustom myself to it'. I wrote:

What an absolute and high standard Brother Lawrence set for himself. I can visualise his life as completely reflecting God's finest nature. I wonder will that ever be possible for me?

In the free hour in the evening after a rapid ten minutes' walk from college, more than sixty of us would gather for Christian fellowship, squeezing in a small building with an earth floor, the men and the girls on opposite sides. Here we realised the presence of God. Our studies and tiredness were forgotten in that vivid hour, when our hearts overflowed.

This last few days the love of the Lord has captured me completely. When I get up, when I go to sleep, when I walk to the lecture room or the laboratories, I have this sense of being wrapped around by his love which is so perfect. I begin to understand what Paul meant when he said God's strength is made perfect in weakness, and his wonderful riches are manifest through our poverty. Our Lord is most wonderful.

I keep thinking about what has happened in the past days and years. It seems there is a thread which goes through all this happiness, and at the end of this I shout with Paul: 'Who can separate us from the love of Christ?'

In our fellowship we sing from Romans 8: 'Shall tribulation, or distress, or persecution, or famine, or nakedness, or peril, or sword ... No, in all these things we are more than conquerors through him who loved us. For I am sure that neither death, nor life, nor angels, nor principalities, nor powers, nor things present, nor things to come, nor height, nor depth, nor anything else in all creation, will be able to separate us from the love of God in Christ Jesus our Lord.' You should hear us singing!

Our leader, by mutual consent, was John, a fellow student who demonstrated Brother Lawrence's experience. When we had gathered for Bible reading John would quietly stand, his eyes sparkling. If it were a prayer night he would silently kneel, and we would follow.

John* was a big husky northerner, older than most of us, in his late twenties I think: a gentle giant. With an absolute disregard of material possessions, he was a gifted leader, of stable temperament and unshakable faith. He was in his third year when I arrived, and I marvelled at his wisdom and maturity.

John set great store, as did other discerning believers, by Wang Ming-dao's *Spiritual Food Quarterly*, with its searching Biblical exposition, challenge and comment. Mr. Wang ministered in the Christian Tabernacle in Peking, but set aside regular times for writing. Thousands discovered Christ through his eloquent preaching, for he was a gifted evangelist. John publicised his Biblical studies.

Wang Ming-dao's troubles with the new government deepened. Mao preferred discussion, criticism, persuasion and education to coercion and repression, a point he made in his speeches, but the Peking preacher failed to respond to what Mao called the democratic methods. So coercion and repression were introduced.

In 1954 the regular supply of *Spiritual Food Quarterly* ceased, and back numbers, skilfully concealed, became like gold. Wang Ming-dao was publicly accused and no printer dared produce his magazine. His name was in newspapers throughout China. To be seen reading him was considered an act of provocation. In 1955 he received a prison sentence.

* Not his real name.

The Christian Tabernacle was closed, but his writings continued to minister grace.

His misfortune did not diminish our regard for him. When John quoted his words we listened even more attentively.

There are Christian leaders who are immaculately dressed. Not so John. His clothes were patched, and his cotton shoes gave poor support, but he was wealthy, in the manner of the Apostle Paul. For the bitter winter evenings he had a thick padded navy blue jacket, which he gathered tightly to himself. There was consternation when he came without it, wearing a thinner, much older garment, woefully inadequate.

'John, where's your jacket?' we demanded, as a terrible suspicion gripped us. He was chilled. Shanghai can be very cold.

He shrugged impatiently, making no reply. 'There are vital matters to concern us,' his eyes said.

Then we knew. It was hard not to be angry, but what could we do with such a man?

He had given the jacket, we later found, to a student from the south, not a member of the fellowship, who possessed no coat. John's chances of obtaining a similar garment were nil, but his action was instinctive.

The months passed. Spring came and went. He was undergoing criticism, facing a harsh ordeal, when the recipient of the coat, still an unbeliever, spoke in his support.

John was the best student in his college year, unusually well endowed with brains, and but for his faith would have been destined for a career of national distinction. In his company we were taller, braver.

He truly practised the presence of God. I valued the choice books Michael had sent to me, but I learned more by observing John. 'It is the lives like stars,' said Phillips Brooks, 'which simply pour down upon us the calm light of their bright and faithful being, out of which we gather the deepest calm and courage. It is good to know that no man or woman can be strong, gentle, good, without somebody being helped and comforted by the very existence of that goodness.'

When I looked at John I saw strength, simplicity, holiness. A book is soon forgotten, but I will not forget him.

How thankful I am that he was in God's school with me. Like Brother Lawrence, 'When the appointed times of prayer were passed, he found no difference, because he still continued with God.'

Meditation

'With what shall I come before the Lord, and bow myself before God on high? Shall I come before him with burnt offerings, with calves a year old? Will the Lord be pleased with thousands of rams, with ten thousands of rivers of oil? Shall I give my first-born for my transgression, the fruit of my body for the sin of my soul?'

He has showed you, O man, what is good; and what does the Lord require of you but to do justice, and to love kindness, and to walk humbly with your God?

Micah 6: 6–8

Lesson Nine

The Wealth of the Church

China is not to be won for Christ by self-seeking, ease-loving men and women. Those not prepared for labour, self-denial, and many discouragements will be poor helpers in the work. In short, the men and women we need are those who will put Jesus, China, souls first and foremost in everything and at all times: life itself must be secondary. . . . Their price is far above rubies.

JAMES HUDSON TAYLOR

IN OUR FELLOWSHIP we put aside certain evenings to study church history, an excellent means of getting a perspective on our own youthful days. We were not brilliantly informed, and I guess we blundered, but we dug into the books we shared. We were frighteningly ignorant of the church in other parts of the world, but we made a discovery that was applicable in every country and every age. Wherever and whenever men took the oath of allegiance to Christ there was a cross. I wrote about it to my brother.

I spent a little time studying church history as this has been a topic among us recently. It is now deeply engraved on my heart that the suffering of Christians has become the wealth of the church. Two years ago I wouldn't have been able to understand this, but it has been the way for nearly 2000 years. It is not for ease and pleasure we are called. God is re-challenging us today. The voice of those who pass into hell and destruction challenge us. God is today calling young people to follow him. My meditation in recent days has been Isaiah 43: 10–12: 'You are my witnesses,' says the Lord, 'and my servant whom I have chosen, that you may know and believe me and understand that I am he. Before me was no god formed, nor shall there be any after me ...'

I added the reports of two examinations: I got 87 out of 100 for embryology and 89 for physiology. The others are yet to come.

One memorable evening our fellowship was addressed by Dr. Yu who had translated *Madame Guyon* by T. C. Upham into Chinese. It was one of our most loved and widely read books. Like other giants of church history Madame Guyon held her life cheap, never shrinking. She had died in June

1717, aged sixty-nine years, after violence and imprisonment, being judged a heretic by the Roman Catholic
church in France of which she was a member. Her pre-
dicament seemed close to ours. We would have welcomed
her in our fellowship. As it was we knew her intimately. We
wished to be loyal to China, as she strove to remain true to
her church; and with what wretched heartache.

For four years, from 1689, she was a prisoner in a tower in
the Bastille. At the base of the tower were the dungeons.
These were below ground level, admitting little or no light.
Above the dungeons rose successively four apartments, all
of which were prisons. In one of these her furniture con-
sisted of a bed, a table, a chair, a basin, and a large earthen
pitcher for holding water, a brass candlestick, a broom, and
a tinder-box. There was no ventilation. She was shut up in
one of these abodes for four years to prevent her making
any further exertions in the cause of Christ.

In a letter written shortly before her removal to the Bastille she said:

> I have no fear of anything but of being left to myself.
> So long as God is with me, neither imprisonment nor
> death will have any terrors. Fear not. If they should pro-
> ceed to extremities and should put me to death, come
> and see me die.

The methods of her captors frequently resembled those of
our interrogators, playing cat and mouse, creating rumours.
She was released in 1707, when she was fifty-four, but only
to begin a long period of banishment in Blois, a city a hundred miles south-west of Paris. During this period she wrote:

> I came out of my place of confinement in the Bastille;
> but, in leaving my prison, I did not leave my cross. My
> afflicted spirit began to breathe and recover itself a little
> after the termination of my residence there; but my body
> was from that time sick and borne down with all sorts of
> infirmities. I have had almost continual maladies, which
> have often brought me to the verge of death.

And later:

> It seems to me that I should be willing, in my own

person, to endure sufferings, if it might be the means of
bringing souls to the knowledge and love of God. I have
but one motive — that of God's glory.

Dr. Yu had long been an admirer of this gallant woman,
but little knew when he made the translation of her biography how pertinent it would be to a group of Chinese
medical students in God's school in Shanghai. He addressed
us on the will of God.

Basing his exposition on Scripture, and using his own experience and that of Madame Guyon by way of illustration,
he told how as we faced the future we must be absolutely
open before God, having no preconceived ideas or choices,
looking only to God to reveal his purpose.

'God,' he said, 'will act on this condition that I must first
of all be willing to do his will. Jesus said, "If any man's will
is to do his will, he shall know." Often we do not know
God's will because we are not willing to do it.'

Were we ready, he asked, like Madame Guyon, to suffer,
to die, to lay down our lives?

I examined my heart. I wanted to be heroic, and to be
honest, I longed to say, 'Ask anything of me, Lord. I will
endeavour to do it'; like Mary of Nazareth to cry, 'Behold,
the handmaid of the Lord; be it unto me according to thy
word.' But was I sure of myself?

The storm clouds had gathered. The evangelistic gather-
ing we had planned had been cancelled. In Shanghai there
were fresh restrictions and terror in many hearts. I informed
Michael:

> We have had to cancel the conference because no place
> is available and no speakers can come. Instead we are
> trying to have some smaller prayer groups meeting at
> different times. We realise more and more how narrow the
> road is and how challenging the cross, and fewer and
> fewer continue to be willing to endure. I ask you to pray
> for these small groups. Although our conference will have
> a new style, surely God intends to bless us just the same.

Four days later I confirmed:

> We have decided to hold three informal prayer fellow-
> ships because all the possibilities for big conferences have

gone. I cannot understand, but some of the older brethren who were to lead us have now said they have no burden to come, so we reckon God is in this. In the prayer fellowships we all ask ourselves one question: 'Am I prepared to offer myself on the altar?' Maybe the cost we are going to pay will be the highest. More and more I realise one cannot serve two masters. God is absolute.

By our suffering would we add to the wealth of the church?

Prayer

> *What thou hast given to me,*
> *Here Lord, I bring to thee,*
> *Feet which must follow thee,*
> *Lips which must sing for thee,*
> *Limbs which must ache for thee,*
> *Ere they grow old.*

Lesson Ten

A Forgiving Heart

Everything seemed to be going wrong: a friend going out into the night to betray him, another drawing a sword in anger, people going into hiding, or running away naked in their eagerness to escape. In the midst of it all Jesus said to those who had come to take him, 'I am he', so peacefully and so quietly that instead of him being nervous it was they who trembled and fell backwards. This was an experience that has been repeated in the martyrs of every age. They could be tortured or burned, but because they possessed his peace, the onlookers could only wonder at their dignity and composure.

WATCHMAN NEE in **Love Not the World**

THERE WAS LITTLE levity but a painstaking resolve among
the students. We saw ourselves as part of a crusade to
bring health and healing on a scale unknown in China.
For us, that crusade started by setting our minds to the task
of learning.

Mao's words were quoted. 'Complacency is the enemy of
study. We cannot learn anything until we rid ourselves of
complacency. Our attitude towards ourselves should be "to
be insatiable in learning" and towards others "to be tireless
in teaching".'

The American preacher, Phillips Brooks, visited a div-
inity school where the men prayed and exhorted one
another, 'their souls exalted and their nature on fire'. The
next day he met some of the same men at a Greek recitation.
'It would be little to say of some of the devoutest of them
that they had not learnt their lessons,' he wrote. 'They had
not got hold of the first principles of hard, faithful, con-
scientious study.'

With the medical opportunities before us we did not
neglect our studies; we strove for excellence, relating our
goals to our natural God-aided powers. Idleness or neglect,
like irritability or pride, reflected on the Gospel. Industry,
effort and effective study methods contributed to success as
well as intelligence and special abilities.

Why scrape through if, with God's help, we could emerge
triumphantly?

A longing for true wisdom found expression in a letter to
Michael at the beginning of the Chinese New Year.

My prayer for this New Year is in the words of Psalm
90: 'Teach us to number our days, that we may get a heart
of wisdom.' I praise the Lord that he has promised in

Psalm 65 to crown the year with grace. I cannot but remember God's many answers to prayer.

I prayed that I should come to Shanghai. He granted. I prayed that I might study medicine. He granted. I prayed that I might be in this particular college. He granted. I hoped to study paediatrics. He granted. Now I am so embarrassed to ask for any more!

How we needed the heart of wisdom. There was, for example, the puzzle of how to deal with Po-ta (I will call him that).

Basically, Po-ta was a bewildered and unstable individual. The cause of his instability was known. His father, a godly man, was serving a long sentence because of his faith. Why had God allowed this? It was a momentous testing for the son.

Po-ta did not speak freely of this, but he was summoned repeatedly to be questioned about his father and those members of his family resident near Shanghai. He would return in an agitated state, with the symptoms of deep anxiety.

He was specialising in surgery, in his third year, and had satisfactory marks from his lecturers.

'What can I do?' he would ask, a worried look on his face. 'Why don't they leave me alone?' His eyes were pitiful. He did not want his father to suffer more on his behalf.

Po-ta's own spiritual experience was genuine. A Christian home had left its happy mark on him, and in our fellowship we had watched his growth in commitment. Yet twice, under pressure, he had deserted us. Twice he had been welcomed back, affectionately, as we shared his grief and assured him of God's pardon.

The second time his stay was short.

In summer, 1955, he faced an ultimatum. The exact details were not known. We saw his pale, tense face. There was a whisper of disquiet, then confirmation that he had denied his faith. Later, in a statement, before the entire student body, he announced how his faith in Christ had been an error attributable to his family background.

His dignity had gone, his interior life had collapsed under

a barrage of threats and persuasion, but we knew not to under-estimate the grace of God.

'I'm no longer a Christian,' he declared to applause. 'My out-dated religion has been replaced by a faith in the People's Republic. I recognise my mistakes, that my faith was an encumbrance. I join the revolution.'

He spoke of his family as reactionaries, of the church which he alleged had carried out treasonable activities under the cloak of religion, and of those who smeared and libelled the People's Government.

A typical confession, prepared under stress, by a young man who did not want to follow his father into a labour camp. There was a pantomime atmosphere about it, but not to us Christians.

'Who's next?' we asked ourselves, grouped together, dazed. Our dismay was not unfounded. As part of his written confession, pages of it, he would have given personal details of us. With dismay we remembered our conversations in his presence, what we had said about our families, even the nature of our prayers and Bible readings. Our dossiers, already substantial, would be fatter.

Knowing his frailty should we have shared so deeply with him? With more wisdom would we have kept him on the fringe? Had we brought misfortune on our own heads?

'Better not trust anyone,' prudence whispered. 'It's the trip to disappointment.'

No, surely not. Po-ta needed the encouragement which came from intimate fellowship, from trust. How could we have excluded him? Jesus had made Judas his treasurer, had given him their tiny resources, although he knew all things from the beginning.

The next days were agony. The small building where we gathered for prayer, our Bethel, was out of bounds. We lived in a huddled attitude. Po-ta was a name we hardly dared breathe. He avoided us, our presence being a rebuke, a reminder of his father, but I had an affection for him.

During a confused period before his denial when I had been retained for indoctrination, and unable to communicate with my friends, he had slipped me a scrap of paper. The scribbled words were a Chinese translation of the hymn:

Not a shadow can rise, not a cloud in the skies,
    But his smile quickly drives it away;
Not a doubt nor a tear, not a sigh nor a fear,
    Can abide while we trust and obey.

After his denial we next met as a fellowship in the attic-room flat of a Christian architect. The taller men had to bend their heads to avoid the sloping roof, but it was a sanctuary.

> And he will show you a large upper room furnished; there make ready ... 'But behold the hand of him who betrays me is with me on the table. For the Son of Man goes as it had been determined; but woe to that man by whom he is betrayed.' And they began to question one another, which of them it was that would do this.

Jesus did not mention Judas because he wished to give each disciple an opportunity of examining himself. In such a crucial hour each man needed self-examination, to search his heart.

John saw us as a family, with an absentee. Knowing our hearts, he reminded us of the words of Jesus: 'Judge not, that you be not judged. For with the judgment you pronounce you will be judged, and the measure you give will be the measure you get. Why do you see the speck that is in your brother's eye, but do not notice the log that is in your own eye?'

His quiet voice and steady faith lessened disquiet and distress, eased the feeling of betrayal, as we stood on the unknown threshold.

'Let's ask our Heavenly Father to give each of us a forgiving heart. We must forgive as Christ forgave us. There must be no bitterness. Betrayed? And so was Christ.'

'Loving God,' my heart cried, 'make me forgiving and give me a heart of wisdom. May I not be cautious when you want me to be vulnerable.'

Prayer

O God, fill us with love, joy, peace, long-suffering, gentleness, goodness, faith, meekness, temperance. May we love those who hate us, forgive those who wrong us, remembering always your goodness and mercy to us. Amen.

Lesson Eleven

How They Love One Another!

Not merely in the words you say,
Not only in your deeds confessed,
But in the most unconscious way
Is Christ expressed.

Is it a beatific smile?
A holy light upon your brow?
Oh no! I felt his presence
When you laughed just now.

To me, 'twas not the truth you taught,
To you so clear, to me still dim,
But when you came you brought
A sense of him.

And from your eyes he beckons me,
And from your heart his love is shed,
Till I lose sight of you and see
The Christ instead.

'LOOK!' SAID THE opponents of the dynamic early Christian church. 'Look how those Christians love one another. Look how they are prepared to die for one another.'

In Christ's work in China there is no more revolutionary force than love. The missionaries in the nineteenth and twentieth centuries discovered this. So did their converts.

After the missionaries had gone, when their sermons were forgotten and their books destroyed, when the churches they had built became welfare centres or museums, when there was little left of the grandiose structures, we remembered their love. The memory lingered like a soothing balm.

There were disgruntled missionaries, soured by disappointment, but they were untypical. Most were loving ambassadors not withered men.

Their charity came to mind when an edict was made, in my third college year, that Christians were not to speak of their faith unless invited to do so. The chance of an invitation was minute. To speak of Christ was to spread reactionary theories; to invite another to do so was considered sick.

The edict appalled us and led to sleepless nights. When we recovered from the initial shock and our numbed senses returned we contemplated our position.

With our voices silenced we would be like freshly arrived missionaries who wanted to communicate but did not speak the language. Loving, serving, praying, being a friend, this would be our sole evangelistic method.

Jesus, in his earthly ministry, gave the perfect demonstration of this outflowing love.

Our own loving was lamentable, but we were to make a discovery: that spartan, humdrum, everyday life offers an endless succession of opportunities to love, to serve, and be a friend.

Let me tell you about Chieh, an ardent member of the communist Youth League, who, like myself, was specialising in paediatrics. We were paired for study. This was to condition my thinking, and allow a watch of my activities.

He had to monitor what I did and said, and where I went. Poor Chieh! It was a thankless task, a tiresome burden, but better to be the reporter, he consoled himself, than the reported.

I did not complain. By nature he was neither vindictive, nor hostile. He borrowed my medical notes and this put him in my debt, a point he presumably did not report, and on which I did not capitalise.

'Tomorrow we start at the children's hospital,' he said, with a flush of enthusiasm.

We were beginning a period of practical duty, an exhilarating prospect, being at minimum a respite from earnest note-taking and revision. A break, too, from autopsies.

Deep feelings flood up in me in a children's ward, with its tiny patients, nervous, confident, happy, home-sick, and unable to articulate their needs, but emotions must be restrained.

'This is to be my specialist field,' I thought as I moved slowly from one little one to another, forgetting the bedside manner, in danger of losing my heart to them all.

With other student doctors I gathered round the impressive consultant as he shared his diagnosis, the x-rays, and gave us the case-history. How proud father would be to see me.

In the hungry lunch queue, with nurses, clerks, technicians and students, the older girl, standing before me glanced in my direction as if we had met before. I did not recognise her. I was impressed with her bearing, neat attire, plaited hair, and serenity.

She smiled, her face glowing.

'You must be a Christian,' she said, with a warm, confident beam. She spoke quietly, but with animation and no effort to conceal.

I nodded. 'And you also,' I said, experiencing a rush of delight at her pure and natural joy in fellowship.

Chieh behind me, his face averted, was listening hard. An unexpected bonus for his rather dull, monotonous reports?

She came closer. 'You're a student,' she observed.' My name is Faith. I'm earning. May I buy you lunch?'

'Oh, no,' I was about to say, for hospital staff were on low wages, but I lacked a friend in the hospital. 'You're very generous,' I said. My own meal ticket could be used later. 'Be my guest another day.'

'We'll lunch again, but do not repay me. This is my pleasure, and I'm employed.'

At a square table I introduced Chieh as my study companion. He acknowledged her with courtesy. Faith was in the laboratories. In minutes we were chatting like old friends. Our Christian love was a bond and, so often misrepresented, we found reassurance together. We arranged to lunch again the next day.

That night when the last child was tucked in, when little eyes closed and the lights dimmed, Chieh and I wrote up medical notes in the cramped room allotted to us. It had been a long, exacting day, responding to the children, doing the chores, backwards and forwards. We reckoned we had tramped several miles.

At this hour hospitals are alike the world over, staff moving soundlessly, a disturbed patient breaking the hush, a bell for bed-pans, but mostly quiet expectancy. In the distance a child's plaintive cry.

We were under the night nurse's authority until midnight, then free to return to college.

My fatigue was defeating me. Chieh was studiously going through his papers, shaming me, but I was too exhausted. In the right-hand pocket of my cotton-jacket I fingered the slim Chinese New Testament.

'Chieh,' I said, hesitantly, 'would you object if I read my Bible?'

He saw I was bone-weary.

'Go ahead,' he said companionably.

The ribbon marker was in the First Epistle of John which I was memorising. The timeless, majestic words quietened me.

That which was from the beginning, which we have heard, which we have seen with our eyes, which we have looked upon and touched with our hands, concerning the word of life — the life was made manifest, and we saw it, and testify to it, and proclaim to you the eternal life which was with the Father and was made manifest to us.

I read on, slowly, reflectively, coming to chapter four, verse nineteen.

We love, because he first loved us. If any one says, 'I love God,' and hates his brother, he is a liar; for he who does not love his brother whom he has seen, cannot love God whom he had not seen. And this commandment we have from him, that he who loves God should love his brother also.

The muted sounds of hospital life came through the door, and my lips formed the words, and my memory struggled to retain them. 'He who loves God should love his brother also.'

Chieh pushed his books aside with a sigh. His day had been equally full. I looked up. Now for the lecture on the ideological goals of China, I thought, happy to listen in return for the concession.

'Finished?' I asked, indicating his closed books.

We normally talked in Mandarin, but tonight he fumbled for words in the Shanghai dialect.

'Why,' he asked wistfully, with no knowledge of the passage I had been reading, 'do you Christians love one another so greatly?'

'Do we?' I asked nonplussed. 'What makes you ask?'

'I've noticed,' he said, casually. 'For example, at the midday meal. You had never met Faith, but she bought you lunch. You talked. I saw your happiness and understanding together.'

Suddenly afraid, I sought an answer, seeing my words in black and white in his next report. 'Wisdom, please,' I prayed, pondering his sincerity.

'I'll explain,' I said guardedly, 'if you'll promise not to report me.'

I regretted my words instantly, hearing myself in displeasure. 'Are you not also one of his disciples, Peter?' 'Will you keep it to yourself if I tell you?' I was afraid to place my trust in God.

His eyes rested steadily on me.

'You're safe,' he said.

My finger was on verse nineteen, of chapter four. 'We love, because he first loved us . . .'

'Read this,' I said. 'I was memorising it.'

In Mandarin he read the verse aloud, scarcely grasping its meaning, his brow puckered. He read it again.

'Explain "He first loved us".'

My spirit lifted. Night nurse, stay away, children don't cry, until I've told him. Nobody come. I've been invited to talk about Jesus. I must not be disturbed.

In simple words, seeking the power of God, I explained what the Apostle Paul called 'the secret and hidden wisdom of God', which none of the rulers understood, 'for if they had, they would not have crucified the Lord of glory'.

'Why did Christ die?' Chieh asked.

The Holy Spirit alone interprets spiritual truth but I took him back to the days when the blood of animals was shed for the forgiveness of sin. So seldom had I been granted such an opportunity that I was not practised, but while the 'word of the cross is folly to those who are perishing, to us who are being saved it is the power of God.'

'Is this why Christians love one another?' he demanded.

I explained how in the Epistle we find that one who is 'born of God' believes (5: 1), and obeys (3: 9), and loves (4: 7). 'All men are selfish, arrogant, petty, but the love of God can make us new creatures.'

He pondered. The world stood still. I stopped talking, to give God a chance, so he could listen to him. Had I confused him, been too anxious? A nurse moved briskly along the corridor.

'I find it difficult to love,' he said. 'I'm suspicious of everyone, choked with hate. I loathe myself. For five years I've been a Youth League member. We don't love each other. We don't trust each other. We pretend.'

It was a staggering confession, with silly risks, possibly an indiscretion.

The night nurse came, her timing perfect.

'It's midnight,' she breathed, glancing in. 'You may go now.'

We gathered our scattered belongings, thrust the books and notes in our bags, and prepared to leave. A new day was beginning.

'May I carry your bag?' Chieh asked.

I could have dropped. In eighteen months it was the first time. Girls like me coped. He reached out. 'Let me take it.'

'No, no, thank you, I'd like to carry it myself,' I said, fearing we might be seen.

The hospital was seven minutes' walk from the college and our dormitories. We did not talk, relishing the fresh night air after the hospital. Chieh broke the silence.

'Tell me more about this love you Christians possess,' he begged.

We stopped under a street light.

'Could I become a Christian, and start loving, not hating?' he asked. 'Like Faith, like you?'

It was Faith's spontaneous love as we queued for our meal which had arrested him. We had not met before, but our oneness in spirit had been evident. A meal ticket, falling like a grain of mustard seed, had triggered off a deep desire.

'Chieh, you can become a Christian now, here,' I said. 'I'll pray with you.'

Standing in the street, in the gentle breeze, our eyes closed, he repeated a prayer after me, confessing his sin, asking forgiveness, seeking to be a child of God. The scent of heaven was in the air.

'I am serious,' he said, when we looked up. There was no reason to doubt it.

'I'll continue to pray for you,' I promised, bidding him goodnight, deliriously happy. 'And others will pray too.'

Chieh needed those prayers. He became one of the reported instead of the reporter. He was dismissed from the communist Youth League, and detained in the college for self-criticism and political study, but he stood manfully, vulnerable, loyal to Christ.

After I left China he married Faith.

Prayer

> So shine in us our little love reproving,
> That souls of men may kindle at the flame;
> The whole world's hatred, broken by our loving,
> Shall bow to love thine everlasting name.

Adapted from a fourth century hymn

Lesson Twelve

God's Perfect Timing

*At one hundred 'his (Abraham's) body was as good as
dead' (Romans 4: 9). There was no longer any way for
him to have a son naturally. Then Isaac came. We too
need to reckon ourselves dead before we can believe
fully in the God who gives life to the dead. Abraham
was shown that he himself was not the father, the source,
of anything. God waits until we have reached an end
of ourselves, and then Isaac comes . . . With Isaac it was
altogether a matter of time – God's time.*

WATCHMAN NEE in **Changed Into His Likeness**

WE MUST LEARN to recognise God's time in our life. It is not easy; but in the summer of 1955 an incident occurred which showed me how his timing is perfect. He is never impatient. He never lags behind.

That summer Christians who had not responded to communist persuasion were detained in college for the holidays, for further indoctrination and self-criticism. 'The mistakes of the past must be exposed without sparing anyone's sensibilities,' Mao ruled. 'Our aim in exposing errors and criticising shortcomings, like that of a doctor curing a sickness, is solely to save the patient and not to doctor him to death.'

'No summer break this year.' The glum news brought despondency. After all that study. How mean!

To face a big trial can be easier than to accept a disappointment like a lost holiday. We surrendered ourselves abjectly, as fellow students packed and left. It was pointless to argue.

A Roman Catholic student, in another college, hanged himself. It unnerved the staff, and put a noose round our necks. Supervision spread, day and night, even to the toilet. The complete lack of privacy added to the state of emotional suspense.

Two tormented brothers, members of our fellowship, after a gruelling interrogation, denied their faith. Their spirits snapped. They were instantly rewarded.

'You may now go on holiday.'

But there was no gaiety in their step as they left. They loathed themselves.

Yet in the night I envied them.

'I want to be free, Lord,' I cried, falsely picturing them in a relaxed holiday mood, absent from this sweltering city.

I have told of my own moment of insanity, how I

disobeyed orders and ran, from the room where I had been under fire, into the rain. 'God, if I deny your name would you not understand?' I cried.

I sympathised with the brothers who had betrayed their Lord. Surely God was not less understanding. I was impoverished by their departure, our ranks were breaking, and I sensed the devil's glee.

A week passed. And a second week. Then the two brothers returned, their heads low, sick with remorse.

'We cannot give up our faith,' they said.

They sought no concession and did not ask what the future held. They barely cared. The momentous news spread.

'How wonderful,' we whispered.

'We can't live without Christ,' the brothers confessed. 'Better to die for him than to exist without him.'

I had written to Michael a little earlier.

We have to pray for each other, because material gain, future prospects, all offer temptations. Everybody tends to dream of beautiful things, but what does the future hold for me? Recently, my meditations have been on how the Lord chose to suffer for our sake; for the joy that was set before him, he endured the cross. Paul has told us that the ultimate end is full of glory.

We don't know when the end will come, but we are told to be watchful. What we have is only today. Yesterday is already passed. Tomorrow is in God's hand.

That year throughout Shanghai and in the cities of China there were bizarre, sombre days for Christians, and examples of spectacular courage.

In Peking, Wang Ming-tao published a pamphlet *We, Because of Faith*. 'Whatever teachings are not in the Bible we totally reject,' he wrote. 'For our loyalty to God we are ready to pay any cost that is required. We shall shrink from no sacrifice. Misrepresentations and slander can never intimidate us.'

The cost was savage. In August he was arrested. No one knew what he went through, but he was made to sign a confession before his release. Broken in mind, he called himself

Peter. When he publicly stated his regret in signing the confession, he went to prison again.

David Adeney, the well-known missionary amongst students said: 'No man had had a greater influence among students than Wang Ming-tao.'

My interrogator was a zealous communist student, who approached me with skill and firmness, and sought initially to be companionable. We were shut up together, myself reluctantly, she by choice, a fine demonstration of dedication.

I sought to influence her for Christ. She would have made a brave disciple, but her displeasure with me multiplied as the days passed. The battle was between two ways of life. She saw my faith stagger but not expire. I tortured myself by wishing to please God and satisfy her.

I had to write an autobiographical essay, giving every memory from the age of eight, naming relatives, friends, neighbours, the elders of the church. The lovely world of childhood memories, of kind deeds and singing birds, was sullied.

'What did your father earn? Was he friendly with the American imperialists? Were they guests in your home? Tell me about your Sunday school teacher. You were converted at a Youth for Christ meeting, and the preacher was an American, Bob Pierce — why when your father was a preacher? When did your father leave home? Did he have a travel permit? Where is he now?'

Eating became an effort, my mind scarcely functioned, I was lifeless, then there was a fresh act of mental violence. I was told to renounce my father. My father!

'How can I?' I protested, bracing myself. 'I love him. He is a good man, a generous man. You would like him,' I dared to venture.

If I denied him life would be less perilous. But what a conscience I would have. He had not flinched or wavered. Dear, dear father.

'You're to declare he's no longer your father,' I was instructed, 'and forever to disassociate yourself from him. You must draw the line to prove your own stand.'

'I cannot. Never!'

'He has betrayed China.'

'He loves China. He would do nothing to harm or disgrace it. He's proud to be Chinese.'

'Then why did he leave?'

'I have explained.'

'Fool,' she snorted. 'Then you will renounce Christ.'

'He is my Saviour,' I replied, remembering the triumphant night of my conversion. I had knelt with fifty or sixty others and made a voluntary vow: 'I will be a Christian all my life, whatever the cost.' A strong, bold prayer, with a background of soft music, on a July night long ago.

My resolve held but my heart was pounding as I cried myself to sleep that night.

'Jesus, it remains my choice to be your disciple. It is my honour. Save me.'

The next day the hours of humiliating terror continued, until my mind fogged. I listened to stories of evil imperialistic missionaries, of their privileged life, of their gross misdeeds. I was told of mission stations which had been spy centres, financed from London or Washington. Senseless, fantastic fabrications.

'See how they defrauded us,' she insisted, mellowing her tone. 'Living in fine homes, comfortably off, collecting money from the poor. Did a missionary ever go hungry?'

Yes, like my father did, but it was pointless to explain. We were not communicating.

'The date of your trial is July 16,' I was told.

My throat was dry. I would face a mass meeting of about one thousand people, including well-wishers, anxious to witness the collapse of my faith. Such gatherings were commonplace. Unless I switched allegiance my studies would terminate and I would be sent away for reform through labour.

My companion grimaced. 'Your future's in your own hands,' she said. She wanted me to recant for my own sake; showing good sense and moderation. She did not like the idea of a labour camp for a fellow medical student. She was not a natural oppressor.

Christlike zeal is tempered by love, but with a zealous communist there is no restraint. When the carrot and the stick fail, the carrot is thrown away.

On the day before my trial God sent a messenger to me.

Normally scrupulous in obeying rules, at nine in the evening my companion left me unattended for a few minutes. I was in a ground-floor room, with opening windows, but an escape attempt would abruptly end my medical career.

I glanced out, praising God for this moment alone, drinking in the peace of it. Striding along the path was a Christian who had greeted me on my first day in college. He was now in his final year. No one was permitted to communicate with me except my interrogator, but perhaps he would smile or wave. His eye swept the grounds, and he made towards me.

'Go away,' I should have shouted, my admiration and fear growing as he came closer. He must avoid association with me. I was out of bounds.

'I'm praying for you,' he whispered through the glass. 'We all are.'

Without a pause my champion strode away. If his heart was quaking he did not show it. His coming had coincided so extraordinarily with my few moments alone. How did he know? Had an angel sent him?

I absolutely glowed. God had not forsaken me as I faced the drama ahead.

Readers of *The Chinese Church That Will Not Die* will know how I was delivered from the mass trial. About 4 a.m. on the night before, I awakened with acute pain. I rolled about to find relief, smothering my groans so as not to disturb my companion. She awoke, took my temperature, and became alarmed.

'Under no circumstances am I supposed to take you to the hospital,' she said. I sipped some water. Between five and five-thirty the pain had become unbearable and she helped me the few minutes' walk to the hospital. At six, despite her protests, the surgeon operated for appendicitis. As the operation was about to begin two medical interns, both Christians, arrived. As the doctor made his critical decision, to operate or not, one of them had awakened with a compulsion to pray for me. He dressed and made his way to emergency and found my name in the admittance register.

God mercifully, lovingly, fixed the hour for my deliverance, and he added grace upon grace by sending two Christian brothers to be with me.

Medical dictionaries record that the appendix, a small, hollow projection from the intestine, serves no useful purpose. Little do the authors know. Three days later I informed Michael:

> I am writing to you from a hospital bed. I have not much to say except that this is one of the wonderful experiences which passes all understanding. God does not allow men to disturb his plan for his children.
>
> I was admitted to hospital as an emergency case. I had told you I was to remain in college for some studies, but three days before I had my operation I began to feel unwell. I once had a grumbling appendix, but did not have treatment because of examinations. During these three days I wanted to endure it without complaining.
>
> By the night of the 15th the pain became so severe that although I did not want to disturb my companion I could not hold on any longer. At 5 a.m. I was taken to casualty.
>
> I found grace before the doctor when he decided to operate on me, and was willing to speak for me. After a very quick preparation the operation took half an hour. I had lumbar anaesthetic and was fully awake.
>
> God was good to me and I am grateful for this experience. Physically, I have never suffered much, but this did me good.
>
> My recent experience is full of grace. I am sorry. I cannot tell you all. I just wish and trust you to understand. Blessed is the one who places his all into the safest hands, and leaves it there without trying to take it back. I am asking the nurse to post this letter.

I also wrote to mother from hospital.

> I cannot imagine what would have happened if I had not been admitted to hospital. I am frightened even to think of this. To me this is a most important lesson. I wish I could tell you more. Those around me are amazed at the wonderful leading of God. As I am quietly resting in hospital I pray for other brothers and sisters who remain in college, that God will not put anything on their shoulders which they cannot bear.

I was discharged from hospital and permitted to go on holiday with no threat overhanging me. My reflections were of God's perfect timetable; copies are not obtainable in advance.

Prayer

Keep me, O Lord, while I tarry on this earth, in a daily serious seeking after thee; that when thou comest, I may be found not hiding my talent, nor yet asleep with my lamp unfurnished; but waiting and longing for my Lord, my glorious God, for ever and ever.

Richard Baxter (1615–1691)

Lesson Thirteen

Not by Bread Alone

What shall we eat? What shall we drink? Wherewithal shall we be clothed? For many these are almost the sole topics of conversation. There is a power that forces you to consider these matters; your very existence demands that you pay attention to them. And yet Scripture warns us that 'the kingdom of God is not eating and drinking, but righteousness' and so on. It bids us first of all seek the kingdom of God and his righteousness, and assures us that as we do so, all these things will be added to us. It bids us be carefree regarding matters of food and clothing, for if God cares for the flowers of the field and the birds of the air, will he not much rather care for us, his own? Yet to judge by our anxieties it would almost seem that they are cared for, but not we!

WATCHMAN NEE in **Love Not the World**

'IS BIG SISTER losing her faith?' my family asked in Hong Kong. 'Is she surrendering?' They examined my letters, which reflected the periods of thought-reform and self-criticism I had undergone. Word had reached them that the assembly which I attended, founded by Watchman Nee, was in disarray. Another of my anchors had gone. On January 21, 1956, the four elders who had been in pastoral charge since his imprisonment were arrested. On January 30, members of the assembly were summoned to a mass denunciation meeting. A few days later about eight hundred Christians gathered in Shanghai, unbelievably, to confirm their approval of Watchman Nee's imprisonment. I wrote home:

> I have seen enough and I am disillusioned; I don't want to ask the opinion of others, or share with them for fear I might be influenced by them and not God alone.

'Yes,' said father. 'Let her be influenced only by God.'
'But,' said Michael, 'she wishes to spend the rest of her life on the mainland. Listen to this.'

> I want to give my life, my training, my profession for my people. I am grateful for the opportunity I have been given, for such a wonderful college, with everything provided. I know I have not failed my people and my country in my studies. Formerly I did not want to link up my faith and my country. Now I have offered all into God's hand. I have a work to do here.

'She can't stay in China,' mother remonstrated. 'She must get out and join us. She belongs with us.'
More alarm bells rang when they received my letter dated March, 1956.

During a series of 'studies' I was very depressed so that I began to put a question mark on my faith. I was fed up with myself and this caused much grief in my heart, but I am glad to say that I have started to distinguish between what is the real faith in Christ, and what are the teachings which are harmful to China. I have come to realise I must not allow anyone to be under the protection of the Christian faith who makes serious criticisms of the new system. These kinds of people should not be in the church of God.

There have been some who have advocated that to be faithful to Christ, one must be cold towards the nation, and refuse to accept the changes that have brought fresh opportunities to China . . .

Previously, I tried to copy an older sister in the assembly, so that I no longer appeared as a young person . . . Maybe some of the older Christians begin to worry about me. I understand. We have to attend many medical seminars and more and more I find how little I know. I thank God we have fine tutors, devoted people, whose life and knowledge challenge me . . .

My family background has affected me considerably, and, of course, all of the past is known to the authorities.

'What does she mean that those who make serious criticisms of the new system should not be in the church of God?' my family puzzled, thinking of godly men in labour camps and prisons, of father himself in exile.

Father said little but stepped up his prayers: 'Protect her, Lord. Keep her for yourself.'

I was now doing clinical subjects, spending more hours in the hospital than the college, even on Sundays. There was extra reading, English books were in circulation again, Russian texts having fallen from favour. I had never grasped Russian, the grammar was too complicated, but English left me completely stranded.

I was part of a research unit, with papers to be written on respiratory diseases. Scientific journals from America and England were imported as part of an advance towards science initiated by the Party.

A few of us sought out Watchman Nee's wife, Charity,

whom he had married in Hangchow in October, 1934. After a period of imprisonment and hospitalisation, she had made her home off Siccawei Road near the college. Because she was classed as a criminal reactionary I could not hint of my contact in letters home. It would have given a measure of reassurance to my parents.

My family's anxiety grew when my letters abruptly ceased. Then rumours reached Hong Kong that this was part of a wider pattern. For six or seven months I was forbidden to send or receive letters. This was to isolate me from treacherous and reactionary thinking.

'It is only forty-five years since the revolution of 1911,' Mao said, 'but the face of China today is completely changed. In another forty-five years, that is in the year 2001, China will have undergone even greater changes. She will have become a powerful, socialist, industrial country. And that is as it should be.'

Between 1952 and 1956 he had been speeding up the socialisation of the countryside. Now over ninety-five per cent of the peasant population were in collectivised farms. He had declared war against famine. Formerly, eighty-five per cent of the population had been engaged in agriculture, but with primitive wooden tools. Away from the towns literacy had been around five per cent. Geologically, the country, with its immense resources, had been unexplored, and heavy industry almost non-existent. Engineers and technicians had been as scarce as doctors.

'Man must eat before he can do anything,' Mao said.

As a Chinese girl I rejoiced that fewer of my people were hungry; that millions were learning to read and write; that the terrible gap between the wealthy and the poor was being closed. I spoke of this in my letters. I had no wish to underestimate the achievement. This new world was thrilling, making the heart beat faster.

It was also dangerous. Father knew this, and so did I, but I had to be restrained in my comment. Not only the family read my letters. Mao had not heeded Christ's words: 'Man shall not live by bread alone . . .' I had been fed, I had been housed, I had been clothed, but there remained a void Mao could not fill.

I hunger and I thirst for thee.

Prayer

> *Like as the hart desireth the waterbrooks,*
> *so longeth my soul after thee, O God.*
> *My soul is athirst for God, yea, even for*
> *the living God; when shall I come to appear*
> *before the presence of God?*
>
> **Psalm 42**

Lesson Fourteen

Our Acceptance

There is no choice;
We cannot say, 'This will I do, or that.'
A hand is stretched to us from out the dark,
Which grasping without question, we are led
Where there is work that we must do for God.

LOWELL

AFTER FOUR YEARS in college, I was to visit my family in Hong Kong. I had formally sought a visa, not daring to hope, haunted by previous turndowns. My mood was subdued as I waited and prayed, concealing my own peculiar agony. When I read it had been granted, and was awaiting collection at the police station, my delight became a fountain.

I bought a two-way ticket. I would return for the one year's practical work prior to my first appointment. Those deadly fourth year examinations were over. The authorities were taking no risk, Shanghai was now my home, and my dream was to be a doctor in my own country.

'God, you are so good to me,' I repeated jubilantly, packing essentials and they, in those days, were few. 'Lord, in black moments, I feared I would not see father again!' I boarded the train for the two-day journey to Hong Kong. The pastures and the woods flashed by, and the busy rivers, as I re-lived the period since father left home on the night of January 2, 1951. Six-and-a-half years. I was reading my Bible when a stern guard passed through the train. He stopped abruptly and gazed with hostility at the book in my hand.

'Put that away,' he ordered curtly.

With Hong Kong a few hours away I did not argue, but his injunction was a sharp reminder of the restrictions placed upon believers. The offence was to read the Bible in a public place.

I was delirious at the prospect of reunion with father, also with mother and Ruby who had been permitted to join him in Hong Kong, and of course with Michael after the letters which had passed between us. I could hardly contain myself. We were thoroughly exhausted when we reached our destination, but the weariness disappeared as the train pulled into the station, and recumbent forms sprang to life.

Before the train stopped I saw Michael, then father, his eyes shining, and a nephew I had not met.

Father had changed little, but in his absence I had passed through my teens. My love, of a small trusting daughter, welled up. What could I do for him? But the request that nearly unbalanced me came from my long-suffering mother.

'Don't return to Shanghai,' she pleaded. 'Stay with us, where you will have a family life, and worship God freely. It'll be a sacrifice professionally, but how I've prayed for this day. You love me, don't you? My heart will break if I lose you. God has not given this deliverance for nothing.'

Father said little but the love in his eyes was as disturbing as mother's words. I was devastated.

'Mother, I love and I respect you.'

'Mary, your place is with us. We're a family that has suffered, that has been separated. Stay with us, please.'

'In China, they're crying out for doctors,' I said gently. 'There are sick children, distraught mothers, who will go untreated. I've got to go back.'

Her lovely face wrinkled. After disappointments, poverty, separation, persecution, the wish was natural. Shanghai was Egypt, Hong Kong the promised land. No one voluntarily returned.

Waves of self-pity washed over me. What a miserable choice. To abandon four years' training? To break mother's heart?

I talked it over with Michael. I repeated what I had written: 'I want to give my life, my training, my profession for my people. I've had a privileged college place. How, as a Christian, can I now abscond?'

Hong Kong was not my promised land. I reacted against the opulence, the greed, the abundance. I saw the nature of the glossy books and magazines on sale, the crude film posters and, disenchanted, questioned the concept of a free world.

I was taken to a store to buy clothes.

'Take your choice,' my companion said.

'All this,' I gasped. 'What a selection.' In Shanghai I had

been allowed three yards of material a year, but nothing so colourful. In the summer I had worn slacks with one of two blouses. In winter, a padded jacket and an outer garment which slipped off for washing. With two of these and a coat I was well clothed.

Now this! It was overpowering, confusing. I was glimpsing a world I did not know existed. After my ordered college life I was insecure, I was with my family but I was a stranger.

After three anxious, fretful weeks, drained of emotion, sympathising with mother's view and dearly loving her, I remained resolute.

'I'm going back,' I announced finally. 'No one, nothing, must prevent me. I'm sorry, mother.'

She was silent as I stood guilty and miserable.

Father, who had been objective, arguing this way, then that, balancing both sides, now came down strongly in support of mother, but until what age, I asked myself, does a child have to obey? For years I had made my own decisions. We might not meet again, that for me too was unbearable, but God would compensate.

And then I had a dream.

In the Old Testament and in the early church God communicated with men through dreams. The story of Joseph and his dreams was among my earliest recollections: 'Behold, I have dreamed another dream; and behold, the sun, the moon, and eleven stars were bowing down to me.' The subject was outside my experience, and had not bothered me because my own dreams were usually a rehash of the previous day's doings and thoughts.

This dream was vivid.

In it I returned to the mainland, and found nowhere to sit or stand in its millions of acres. I moved across miles and miles of fields, over vast rivers, high mountains, and many residences, but there was no place for me. Not a square yard in the whole of China to put down my feet and rest. I awoke with a racing heart, and opened my eyes relieved to find I was still in Hong Kong.

Had God spoken?

The day came for my departure. I made no effort to leave. Before the dream I had refused to accept my family's advice, but I let the train and the day go. I was deep in a valley dark as death.

Outside China my medical training would not be recognised. To be a doctor I would have to commence studies again, with new text books, different professors, fresh examinations. I did not have the will, the resources, the opportunity.

Grey days followed when I was engulfed by fatigue, in a state of lethargy. I had taken a costly training, occupied a valued place, and then deserted. I wrote to the college and swiftly received a letter instructing me to return or be expelled. If I remained an absentee the record of my studies would be destroyed.

When night had settled, and I was alone, my selfish thoughts took over, and I relived months of study — all apparently wasted.

But were they? Had God some purpose?

Elisabeth Elliot in *These Strange Ashes* tells of a blinding disappointment. Marcario, her trusted colleague in translating the Bible into the Colorado language, was shot. He was indispensable to her. Was this an example of how God answered her prayer for his work? He was the key to the whole of the language work and now he was dead. It was her first experience of having to bow down before that which she could not explain. Before, she had simply ignored the unexplainable, occupying her mind with other things, sweeping it under the rug, evading the questions. Now, exactly like myself, she had to face the issue. 'It was a long time before I came to the realisation that it is in our *acceptance* of what is given that God gives himself,' she writes.

In our acceptance? I went to medical school to become a doctor. My hopes were dashed. My training was not recognised outside China. The college became God's school for me, where I struggled with his lessons, where I took the first tottering steps towards Christian maturity. But the stiffest lesson came when I left, never to return. 'In our acceptance of what is given, God gives himself.'

Prayer

O God, when we are faced with the unexplainable, when we are called upon to relinquish, open not only our hand but our heart also; that in our acceptance we may find you; through Jesus Christ our Lord.

Lesson Fifteen

For What Purpose?

We have determined by God's grace to live according to the revolutionary teaching of our Master. Every petty, personal desire must be subordinated to the supreme task of reaching the world for Christ. We are debtors. We must not allow ourselves to be swept into the soul-binding curse of modern-day materialistic thinking and living. The propagation of the faith we hold supreme! Christ is worthy of our all: we must be ready to suffer for him and count it joy, to die for him and count it gain. In the light of the present spiritual warfare, anything less than absolute dedication must be considered insubordination to our Master and mockery of his cause!

George Verwer in **Come, Live, Die**

As THE WEEKS passed I was appalled by what I saw in Hong Kong. There were greedy opportunists at every street corner, and even believers appeared to have accepted non-Christian standards of acquisitiveness.

In Shanghai there had been a fine sense of purpose, of being drilled for a destiny, not only among college students, but throughout the community. There was a splendid and massive urgency, with a succession of aims and challenges, national and individual.

The body was exercised to be fit to defend the country. Men toiled long hours in their enthusiasm. People were doctored to make them well, and to take their place in the march of history. Purposeless monotony had been swept away. True, for some life was harsh, with little enough nourishment, but life in China had never been comfortable for millions.

Hong Kong had its virtues but it was shamelessly indulgent. It had its poverty, its unemployment, its housing problem, alongside the astonishing gadgets of the twentieth century, but money, sex and selfishness flashed from every hoarding.

The absence of purpose was apparent in some Christian circles. Hymns, prayers, discussion and friendship, but the trumpet sound was muffled.

There was less fear and less faith.

Should a Christian be less committed than a communist? A young American was converted to communism in Mexico. He wrote to tell his fiancée the political reason why he was breaking off their engagement.

A certain percentage of us get killed and imprisoned. We live in virtual poverty. We turn back to the Party every penny we make above what is absolutely necessary to keep us alive. We communists don't have the time or the money for many movies or concerts, a T-bone steak or decent homes or new cars. We've been described as fanatics. Our lives are dominated by one great over-shadowing factor, the struggle for world communism. We communists have a philosophy of life which no amount of money could buy.

He continued about a cause to fight for; of subordinating petty personal selves into a great movement of humanity. The one thing of which he was in earnest was the communist cause.

I had seen thousands of young men and women like him. The words of Mao rang in their ears: 'Be resolute, sacrifice, surmount every difficulty ... Courage in battle, no fear of fatigue, and continuous fighting ... Oppose extravagant eating and drinking and pay attention to thrift and economy ... Communists should be the most far-sighted, the most self-sacrificing, the most resolute.'

Challenging, stirring words. If a political philosophy so inspired a man, how much more the Son of God. Born in a cattleshed, trained as a carpenter, he became a preacher in a remote country and died on a criminal's cross. No rank, no privilege, no benefits. Mao, listen: he was 'the most far-sighted, the most self-sacrificing, the most resolute'. He knew blood and tears. He died for our sins. He rose from the dead. Forgive us if we have failed to portray, to exhibit in our lives, the Risen Saviour. Forgive us, God, if men have turned to communism because they only saw disillusioned, disheartened, self-seeking followers of Jesus. Christians without marching orders. Christians without a cross.

A Canadian minister reminds us that most systems revolve around symbols: the crescent, the sickle, the lotus flowers, the spinning wheel, the sun's disc, the living flame; but that Christianity is unique in that it revolves around a cross. Paul wrote to the Corinthians: 'But we preach Christ crucified, unto the Jews a stumbling block, and unto the Greeks foolishness; but unto them which are called, both Jews and Greeks, Christ the power of God, and the wisdom of God.'

If we remove the cross there is no Gospel. The Lord Jesus

who died on that cross said: 'If any man would come after me, let him deny himself and take up his cross and follow me.'

The communists in college were not slow to admire the spirit of dedication and discipline in our fellowship.

'You'd make excellent Party members,' they said, 'if you'd disown God.'

We lived sacrificially. Knowing our supreme commission we were unwilling to be shamed by Party members. Mao said: 'A good comrade is one who is more eager to go where the difficulties are greater.' If there was a tough call we might shrink but as Christians we sought to be there.

In this privileged free world, and how great in its benefits, we have lost the vision, the infectious enthusiasm, the quality of living, which should distinguish us from our pleasure-loving neighbours.

The best of my colleagues in Shanghai were able to say:

> Send me anywhere, only go with me.
> Put any burden on me, only sustain me.
> Sever any earthly tie, save that which
>   binds my heart to thee.

Prayer

> *From subtle love of softening things*
> *From easy choices, weakenings,*
>   *(Not thus are spirits fortified*
>   *Not this way went the Crucified)*
> *From all that dims thy Calvary,*
> *O Lamb of God, deliver me.*
>   Amy Wilson Carmichael

Lesson Sixteen

A Privileged Pupil

Lord, I've muffed it again!
I'm just a dunce in your school.
  I knew I had failed,
  and you knew it too,
  but you said nothing.
Have patience with me!
I'm always going over the same old lessons
  and never really learning them.

I was so sure I could handle that situation.
  I've had plenty of experience of it
  and through trial and error have learnt what
  not to do,
  so I had the theory all right.

I'm sure that if you tested me in theory only
  I could make a better showing.
  But you are not satisfied with theory.
  You insist upon practice,
  and that is where I fail.

Why, Lord, should there be such a gulf fixed
  between theory and practice?
  To know what to do
  and yet not to do it;

to see the pitfalls
and yet stumble into them?

Do you tire of having such a poor pupil,
and feel like washing your hands of me?
Give me another chance!
Perhaps you can show me a better way to learn my
lessons,
so that I don't fail so often.
I want to learn, I really do.
I'm beginning to see that the secret is
to keep in close touch with you,
rather than to rely on theoretical knowledge
or my own endeavours.

Flora Larsson

GOD HAS OPENED wonderful doors for me: doors to churches and homes of God's people across the world; doors to schools and colleges, to share and to laugh with young people; doors to lunch hour meetings of government officers and businessmen and, most of all, doors into the hearts of my affectionate friends and prayer-partners in so many countries.

Wherever I go, whatever I do, I am still a pupil, still failing, still learning. Flora Larsson's prayer-poem *A Dunce In Your School* sums up how I feel when lessons have to be repeated because I did not grasp them.

I count it a privilege to represent the Chinese Christians who cannot be seen, who cannot be heard, who are often forgotten. I am an inadequate representative of those medical students, long qualified as doctors, who remain in China. I was not permitted to return to Shanghai, but out of my deepest disappointment, out of my confusion, I have found God's purpose.

Did God make a mistake? For this public role why did he not select John, our group leader, with his organising ability, a powerful speaker and evangelist? There can be only one answer. There was a bigger job for John. As a doctor in China? As a witness to a living Christ? In a labour camp? God makes no mistakes.

I hesitated long over this book, as I do over invitations to speak, yet by writing and by speaking I am told I can best stimulate your prayers for my former companions. How those prayers are needed! I fear to give information that may harm them, but my prayer is that young people, Chinese and non-Chinese, will be challenged by the story of those I studied with, by the Christians who still worship, often secretly, in China today.

I am able to travel where they cannot go, to boldly declare

what they cannot mention. While their voice is silenced I must speak on their behalf. This, I believe, is God's purpose in permitting my freedom. What a responsibility, what a privilege is mine!

One day, in Heaven or on earth, we will sit with these Christians and share our discovery of the love of God. We will not make speeches; we will laugh, we will sing, we will worship our God Almighty, King of all the earth.

I dream that I am back in Shanghai, or sometimes in Tibet, with the other students. I have found a corner. I sit down quickly, sensing time is scarce, share a few words, then get up and go. But what joy to be there for those fleeting moments.

When I am travelling on a journey, a place or a person reminds me of an event or a believer in China. Is he still serving God? I dismiss the question. Instead I pray for him. I see their faces, but cannot recall their names, or I remember their names, but cannot see their faces. But God forgets neither a face nor a name.

In a tiny church in a village in Norway, in sight of the mountains, with the tang of pine in the air, I was approached by a small, neatly dressed lady. There was love in her eyes.

'I've prayed for China for forty-six years,' she said, scanning my Chinese features, 'and Mary, I am still praying.'

She had prayed for me, with the millions in my country, since before I was born.

'And I am still praying.' The Japanese occupation, the communist takeover, the 1966 cultural revolution, nothing had been able to stop her intercession. She was an old lady. Will you take up her burden? Will you pray for China, and for those Christians who remain there in God's school? I was a dunce, not always learning my lessons, but what a joy to be in his school. I was indeed a privileged pupil.

Action

For information about the Chinese Overseas Christian Mission please write to:

    4 Earlsfield Road,
    London SW18 3DW.